KIM WILDE

All The Top 40 Hits

Craig Halstead

Copyright © Craig Halstead 2020

All rights reserved. No part of this publication may be reproduced, stored in a retrieval system, or transmitted in any form or by any means, electronic, mechanical, photocopy, recording or otherwise, without prior written permission of the copyright owner. Nor can it be circulated in any form of binding or cover other than that in which it is published and without similar condition including this condition being imposed on a subsequent purchaser.

First Edition

for Aaron

BY THE SAME AUTHOR ...

Christmas Number Ones

This book details the Christmas No.1 singles in the UK from 1940 to date, and also reveals the Christmas No.2 single and Christmas No.1 album. The book also features the Christmas No.1s in five other countries, namely Australia, Germany, Ireland, the Netherlands and the USA, and is up-dated annually in January.

The 'All The Top 40 Hits' Series

This series documents, in chronological order, all the Top 40 Hit Singles and Albums by the featured artist:

ABBA
Annie Lennox
Blondie
Boney M.
Carpenters
Chi-Lites & Stylistics
Donna Summer
Janet Jackson
Michael Jackson
The Jacksons
(Jackson 5 / Jackson / Jermaine / La Toya / Rebbie / 3T)
Olivia Newton-John
Sam Cooke & Otis Redding
Tina Turner
Whitney Houston

The 'For The Record' Series

The books in this series are more comprehensive than the 'All The Top 40 Hits' volumes, and typically include: The Songs (released & unreleased), The Albums, The Home Videos, The TV Shows/Films, The Concerts, Chartography & USA/UK Chart Runs, USA Discography & UK Discography.

Donna Summer
Janet Jackson
Michael Jackson
Whitney Houston

ACKNOWLEDGEMENTS

I would like to thank Chris Cadman, my former writing partner, for helping to make my writing dreams come true. It's incredible to think how far we have come, since we got together to compile 'The Complete Michael Jackson Discography 1972-1990', for Adrian Grant's *Off the Wall* fan magazine in 1990. Good luck with your future projects, Chris ~ I will look forward to reading them!

Chris Kimberley, it's hard to believe we have been corresponding and exchanging chart action for 30+ years! A big thank you, I will always value your friendship.

I would like to thank the online music community, who so readily share and exchange information at: Chartbusters (chartbusters.forumfree.it), ukmix (ukmix.org/forums), Haven (fatherandy2.proboards.com) & Buzzjack (buzzjack.com/forums). In particular, I would like to thank:

- 'BrainDamagell' & 'Wayne' for posting current Canadian charts on ukmix;
- 'flatdeejay' & 'ChartFreaky' for posting German chart action, and 'Indi' for answering my queries regarding Germany, on ukmix;
- 'mario' for posting Japanese chart action, and 'danavon' for answering my queries regarding Japan, on ukmix;
- 'Davidalic' for posting Spanish chart action on ukmix;
- 'Shakyfan', 'CZB', 'beatlened' & 'trebor' for posting Irish charts on ukmix;
- 'janjensen' for posting Danish singles charts from 1979 onwards on ukmix;
- 'Hanboo' for posting and up-dating on request full UK & USA chart runs on ukmix. R.I.P., Hanboo, your posts on ukmix are sadly missed;

If you can fill any of the gaps in the chart information in this book, or have chart runs from a country not already featured in the book, I would love to hear from you. You can contact me via email at: **craig.halstead2@ntlworld.com** ~ thank you!

CONTENTS

INTRODUCTION	7
ALL THE TOP 40 SINGLES	17
THE ALMOST TOP 40 SINGLES	98
KIM'S TOP 25 SINGLES	100
SINGLES TRIVIA	104
ALL THE TOP 40 ALBUMS	115
KIM'S TOP 15 ALBUMS	179
ALBUMS TRIVIA	181

INTRODUCTION

Kim Wilde, as Kim Smith, was born on 18th November 1960 in Chiswick, Middlesex, England. She was born into a musical family.

Kim's father, Reginald Leonard Smith, found fame in the late 1950s and early 1960s as Marty Wilde, scoring numerous hits such as *Endless Sleep*, *Donna*, *A Teenager In Love*, *Rubber Ball* and *Sea Of Love*. Her mother, Joyce Baker, sang in the popular vocal trio The Vernon Girls.

Kim was the first of four children, and was followed by brother Richard (known as Ricky) in 1961, sister Roxanne in 1979 and brother Marty, Jr. in 1983.

'It was always very musical in our house,' said Kim. 'Dad would play the guitar and we would join in and sing along.'

Kim was nine when the Smith family moved to Hertfordshire, England, and eleven years later she completed a foundation course at the St Albans College of Art & Design. Around the same time, her brother Ricky bought some studio time at producer Mickie Most's RAK Studio, to record some of his newly penned songs. Kim tagged along, to help out with backing vocals, and it was Mickie Most's wife Chris who first noticed Kim.

'She saw me walking out of the RAK offices,' said Kim, 'and thought I looked like a pop star, which I suppose I did, because I had red and black stripy pants, spiky blonde hair, quite punky looking.'

Ricky released several singles in the early 1970s, including *Do It Again*, *A Little Bit Slower*, *I Am An Astronaut*, *Teen Wave* and *April Love*, but unlike his dad Marty he failed to achieve any notable chart success.

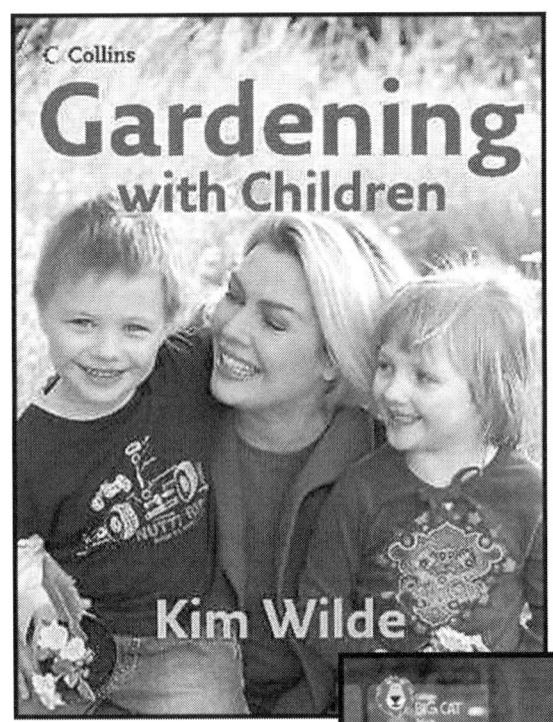

Kim was signed to the RAK record label by Mickie Most. Her debut single, *Kids In America*, was written for her by her father Marty and brother Ricky, with Ricky also producing the recording.

Released in January 1981, *Kids In America* got Kim's career as a singer off to a flying start, rising to no.2 in the UK, and proving popular in many European countries; it even giving Kim her first Hot 100 success in the United States.

The hits kept on coming, and in 1983 Kim won a prestigious BRIT Award, for Best British Female Solo Artist. Five years later, she played 33 dates supporting Michael Jackson, on the European leg of his mega-successful Bad Tour.

Between March 1996 and February 1997, Kim co-starred as Mrs Walker in London's West End production of the The Who's rock musical, *Tommy*, staged at the Shaftesbury Theatre. Here she met co-star Hal Fowler, and the couple married on 1st September 1996, with Kim making public her desire to start a family.

While she was pregnant with her first child, Kim put her musical career on hold, and attended a course in horticulture at Capel Manor college, as she was keen to learn how to create a garden for her children.

Kim's son Harry Tristan was born in January 1998, with her daughter Rose Elizabeth following two years to the month later.

Kim's interest in horticulture led to Channel 4 asking her to act as a celebrity gardener, for their *Better Gardens* programme. This led to numerous other TV and radio gardening-related appearances, including two series of *Garden Invaders* for the BBC.

In 2005, Kim was chuffed to win a prestigious Gold medal award at the Royal Horticultural Society's annual Chelsea Flower Show, for her Cumbrian Fellside garden – a homage to the Lake District. The same year, her first gardening book *Gardening With Children* was published.

'It's based on my own experiences with our children, Harry and Rose,' said Kim. 'It's taken a year to put together and is my first book.'

Other gardening publications followed, including *The First-Time Gardener* and *Harry's Garden*.

Alongside her second career in horticulture, Kim has continued to make new music and perform live, and her 14th studio album *HERE COME THE ALIENS* was released as recently as 2018.

All The Top 40 Hits

For the purposes of this book, to qualify as a Top 40 hit, a single or album must have entered the Top 40 singles/albums chart in at least one of the following countries: Australia, Austria, Belgium, Denmark, Finland, France, Germany, Ireland, Italy, Japan, the Netherlands, New Zealand, Norway, South Africa, Spain, Sweden, Switzerland, the United Kingdom, the United States of America and Zimbabwe (formerly Rhodesia).

The Top 40 singles and albums are detailed chronologically, according to the date they first entered the chart in one or more of the featured countries. Each Top 40 single and album is illustrated and the catalogue numbers and release dates are detailed for the UK, followed by the chart action in each featured country, including any chart re-entries. Where full chart runs are unavailable, peak position and weeks on the chart are given.

For both singles and albums, the main listing is followed by 'The Almost Top 40 Singles/Albums', which gives an honorable mention to Kim's singles/albums that peaked between no.41 and no.50 in one or more countries. There is also a points-based list of Kim's Top 25 Singles and Top 15 Albums, plus a fascinating 'Trivia' section at the end of each section which looks at Kim's most successful singles and albums in each of the featured countries.

The Charts

The charts from an increasing number of countries are now freely available online, and for many countries it is possible to research weekly chart runs. Although this book focuses on Top 50 hits, longer charts runs are included where available, up to the Top 100 for countries where a Top 100 or longer is published.

Nowadays, charts are compiled and published on a weekly basis – in the past, however, some countries published charts on a bi-weekly or monthly basis, and most charts listed far fewer titles than they do today. There follows a summary of the current charts from each country featured in this book, together with relevant online resources and chart books.

Australia
Current charts: Top 100 Singles & Top 100 Albums.
Online resources: current weekly Top 50 Singles & Albums, but no archive, at **ariacharts.com.au**; archive of complete weekly charts from 2001 to 2019 at

pandora.nla.gov.au/tep/23790; searchable archive of Top 50 Singles & Albums dating back to 1988 at **australian-charts.com**.
Books: 'Australian Chart Book 1970-1992' & 'Australian Chart Book 1993-2009' by David Kent.

Austria
Current charts: Top 75 Singles & Top 75 Albums.
Online resources: current weekly charts and a searchable archive dating back to 1965 for singles and 1973 for albums at **austriancharts.at**.

Belgium
Current charts: Top 50 Singles & Top 200 Albums for two different regions, Flanders (the Dutch speaking north of the country) and Wallonia (the French speaking south).
Online resources: current weekly charts and a searchable archive dating back to 1956 for singles and 1995 for albums at **ultratop.be**.
Book: '*Het Belgisch Hitboek – 40 Jaar Hits In Vlaanderen*' by Robert Collin.
Note: the information in this book for Belgium relates to the Flanders region.

Denmark
Current Charts: Top 40 Singles & Albums.
Online resources: weekly charts at **hitlisten.nu**, and formally an archive dating back to 2001 at **danishcharts.com**. No archive currently exists for charts before 2001. 'CZB' has posted weekly Top 20s from September 1994 to December 1999 on **ukmix.org**, and 'janjensen' has posted singles charts from January 1977 onwards on the same forum.
Note: The information in this book is for the singles chart only.

Finland
Current charts: Top 20 Singles & Top 50 Albums.
Online resources: current weekly charts and a searchable archive dating back to 1995 at **finnishcharts.com**.

France
Current charts: Top 200 Singles & Top 200 Albums.
Online resources: current weekly and archive charts dating back to 2001 can be found at **snepmusique.com**; a searchable archive dating back to 1984 for singles and 1997 for albums is at **lescharts.com**; searchable archive for earlier/other charts at **infodisc.fr**.
Book: '*Hit Parades 1950-1998*' by Daniel Lesueur.
Note: Compilation albums were excluded from the main chart until 2008, when a Top 200 Comprehensive chart was launched.

Germany
Current charts: Top 100 Singles & Top 100 Albums.
Online resources: current weekly and archive charts dating back to 1977 can be found at **offiziellecharts.de/charts**.

Books: '*Deutsche Chart Singles 1956-1980*', '*Deutsche Chart Singles 1981-90*' & '*Deutsche Chart Singles 1991-1995*' published by Taurus Press.

Ireland
Current charts: Top 100 Singles & Top 100 Albums.
Online resources: current weekly charts are published at IRMA (**irma.ie**); there is a searchable archive for Top 30 singles (entry date, peak position and week on chart only) at **irishcharts.ie**; an annual Irish Chart Thread has been published annually from 2007 to date, plus singles charts from 1967 to 1999 and album charts for 1993, 1995-6 and 1999, have been published at ukmix (**ukmix.org**); weekly album charts from March 2003 to date can be found at **acharts.us/ireland_albums_top_75**.
Note: the information presented in this book is for singles only..

Italy
Current charts: Top 100 Singles & Top 100 Albums.
Online resources: weekly charts and a weekly chart archive dating back to 2005 at **fimi.it**; a searchable archive of Top 20 charts dating back to 2000 at **italiancharts.com**; pre-2000 information has been posted at ukmix (**ukmix.org**).
Books: *Musica e Dischi Borsa Singoli 1960-2019* & *Musica e Dischi Borsa Album 1964-2019* by Guido Racca.
Note: as the FIMI-Neilsen charts didn't start until 1995, the information detailed in this book is from the Musica & Dischi chart.

Japan
Current charts: Top 200 Singles & Top 300 Albums.
Online resources: current weekly charts (in Japanese) at **oricon.co.jp/rank**; selected information is available on the Japanese Chart/The Newest Charts and Japanese Chart/The Archives threads at **ukmix.org**.

Netherlands
Current charts: Top 100 Singles & Top 100 Albums.
Online resources: current weekly charts and a searchable archive dating back to 1956 for singles and 1969 for albums at **dutchcharts.nl**.

New Zealand
Current charts: Top 40 Singles & Top 40 Albums.
Online resources: current weekly charts and a searchable archive dating back to 1975 at **nztop40.co.nz**.
Book: 'The Complete New Zealand Music Charts 1966-2006' by Dean Scapolo.

Norway
Current charts: Top 20 Singles & Top 40 Albums.
Online resources: current weekly charts and a searchable archive dating back to 1958 for singles and 1967 for albums at **norwegiancharts.com**.

South Africa
Current charts: no official charts.
Online resources: none known.
Book: 'South Africa Chart Book' by Christopher Kimberley.
Notes: the singles chart was discontinued in early 1989, as singles were no longer being manufactured in significant numbers. The albums chart only commenced in December 1981, and was discontinued in 1995, following re-structuring of the South African Broadcasting Corporation.

Spain
Current charts: Top 50 Singles & Top 100 Albums.
Online resources: current weekly charts and a searchable archive dating back to 2005 at **spanishcharts.com**.
Book: *'Sólo éxitos 1959-2002 Año a Año'* by Fernando Salaverri.

Sweden
Current charts: Top 60 Singles & Top 100 Albums.
Online resources: current weekly charts and a searchable archive dating back to 1975 at **swedishcharts.com**.

Switzerland
Current charts: Top 75 Singles & Top 100 Albums.
Online resources: current weekly charts and a searchable archive dating back to 1968 for singles and 1983 for albums at **hitparade.ch**.

UK
Current Charts: Top 100 Singles & Top 200 Albums.
Online resources: current weekly and archive charts dating back to 1960 at **officialcharts.com**; weekly charts are posted on a number of music forums, including ukmix (**ukmix.org**), Haven (**fatherandy2.proboards.com**) and Buzzjack (**buzzjack.com**).
Note: weekly Top 200 album charts are only available via subscription from UK ChartsPlus (**ukchartsplus.co.uk**).

USA
Current charts: Hot 100 Singles & Billboard 200 Albums.
Online resources: current weekly charts are available at **billboard.com**, however, to access Billboard's searchable archive at **billboard.com/biz** you must be a subscriber; weekly charts are posted on a number of music forums, including ukmix (**ukmix.org**), Haven (**fatherandy2.proboards.com**) and Buzzjack (**buzzjack.com**).
Note: older 'catalog' albums (i.e. albums older than two years) were excluded from the Billboard 200 before December 2009, so the chart didn't accurately reflect the country's best-selling albums. Therefore, in this book Billboard's Top Comprehensive Albums chart has been used from December 2003 to December 2009, as this did include all albums. In

December 2009 the Top Comprehensive Albums chart became the Billboard 200, and Billboard launched a new Top Current Albums chart – effectively, the old Billboard 200.

Zimbabwe
Current charts: no official charts, and no known online resources.
Books: 'Zimbabwe Singles Chart Book' & 'Zimbabwe Albums Chart Book' by Christopher Kimberley.
Note: Zimbabwe was, of course, known as Rhodesia before 1980, but the country is referred to by its present name throughout this book.

Notes:

- In the past, there was often one or more weeks over Christmas and New Year when no new album chart was published in some countries. In such cases, the previous week's chart has been used to complete a chart run. Similarly, where a bi-weekly or monthly chart was in place, for chart runs these are counted at two and four weeks, respectively.

- No singles or albums by Kim Wilde have charted in Spain.

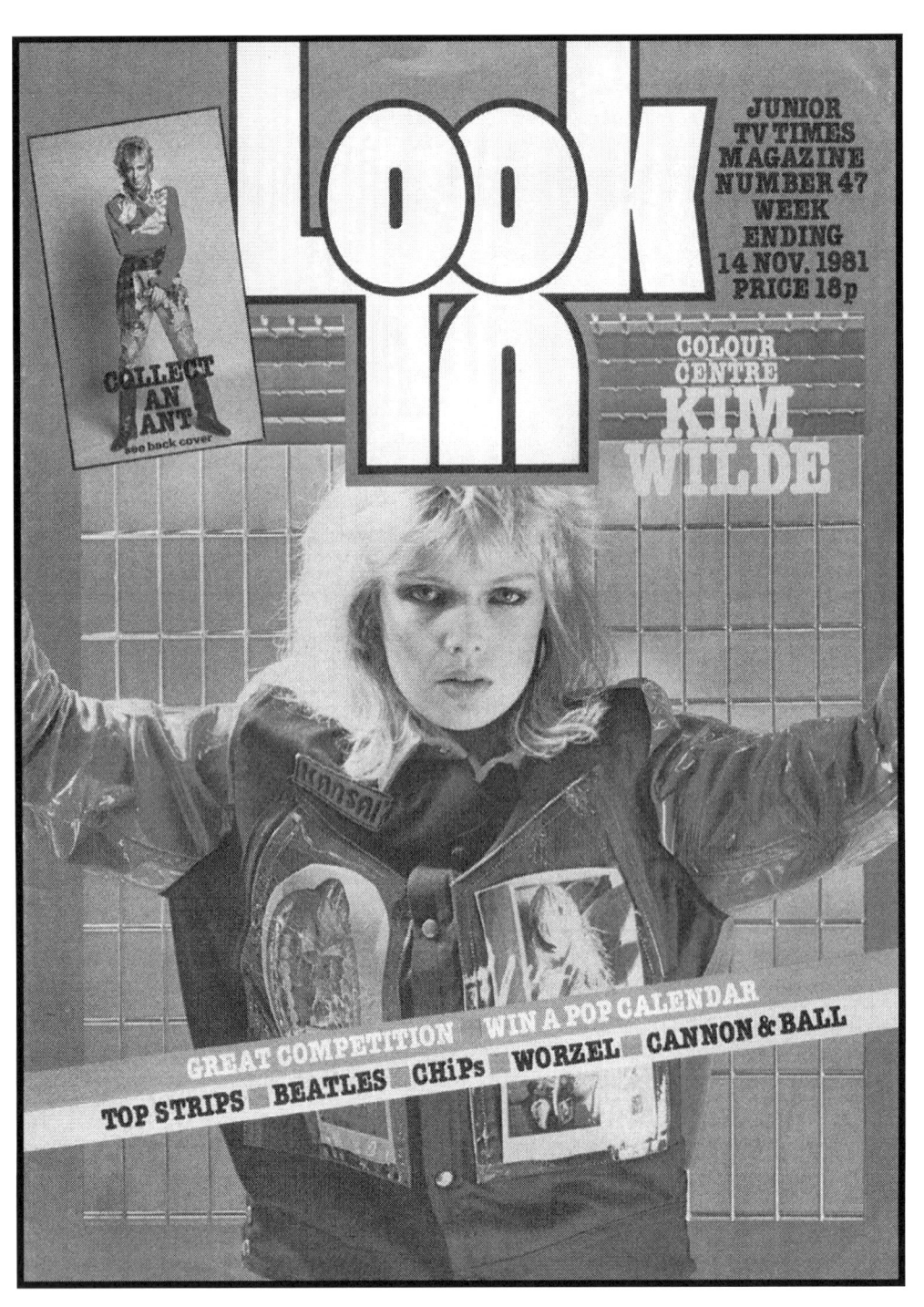

All The Top 40 Singles

1 ~ Kids In America

UK: RAK RAK 327 (1981).
B-side: *Tuning In Tuning On*.

21.02.81: 62-43-18-6-3-**2**-**2**-4-11-14-23-43-60

Pos	LW	Title, Artist		Peak Pos	WoC
1	2 ↑	THIS OLE HOUSE SHAKIN' STEVENS	EPIC	1	5
2	3 ↑	KIDS IN AMERICA KIM WILDE	RAK	2	6
3	1 ↓	JEALOUS GUY ROXY MUSIC	EG	1	6
4	8 ↑	FOUR FROM TOYAH (EP) TOYAH	SAFARI	4	7
5	4 ↓	KINGS OF THE WILD FRONTIER ADAM & THE ANTS	CBS	2	11

Australia
4.05.81: peaked at no.**5**, charted for 25 weeks

Austria
15.07.81: 14-19-**12**-20 (bi-weekly)

Belgium
18.04.81: 39-19-14-10-7-6-**4**-5-6-6-12-14-23

Denmark
24.04.81: 10-9-?-10-4-4-**3**-4-?-7-6-7-9-11-9-9-x-7-12

Finland
04.81: peaked at no.**1** (2), charted for 26 weeks

France
3.04.81: peaked at no.**3**, charted for 44 weeks

Germany
13.04.81: 23-16-12-13-10-8-10-8-9-8-9-11-6-6-**5-5**-10-9-8-9-16-16-15-19-26-34-31-50-49-64-60-71

Ireland
15.03.81: 10-**2**-3-**2-2**-3-4-11-21

Netherlands
25.04.81: 32-24-26-19-12-11-**8**-9-10-13-15-16-26-29

New Zealand
19.07.81: 29-20-14-9-**5-5**-8-6-13-10-25-19-39-40

Norway
1.08.81: **9**

South Africa
28.06.81: peaked at no.**1** (1), charted for 15 weeks

Sweden
24.04.81: 17-3-**2-2**-3-3-3-8-9 (bi-weekly)

Switzerland
24.05.81: 15-9-6-6-6-6-**5**-6-9-10-11

USA
22.05.82: 88-78-64-56-50-47-43-41-37-34-30-26-**25-25-25-25**-85-93

Zimbabwe
3.10.81: peaked at no.**1** (1), charted for 17 weeks

When he heard her singing backing for her brother Ricky, RAK's Mickie Most expressed an interest in working with Kim.

With an intro inspired by Gary Numan, and a synth line influenced by *Messages* by Orchestral Manoeuvres in the Dark, Ricky set about writing a song for Kim on his WASP synthesizer. Dad Marty penned the lyrics, but he only completed the chorus when they were actually in the studio, recording the song that became *Kids In America*.

Mickie Most liked *Kids In America*, but after he and Ricky remixed it, the track was shelved for twelve months. The song was finally released as a single in January 1981, and it got Kim's career off to an explosive start.

'I knew it was a hit,' said Kim. 'The record was all quick-quick-quick. Ricky and my father wrote it quite quickly, it was demoed quickly, and went up the chart quickly.'

In the UK, *Kids In America* rose to no.2 for two weeks, but it was kept off the top spot by *This Ole House* by Shakin' Stevens. The single did go all the way to no.1 in Finland, South Africa and Zimbabwe, and achieved no.2 in Ireland and Sweden, no.3 in Denmark and France, no.4 in Belgium, no.5 in Australia, Germany, New Zealand and Switzerland, no.8 in the Netherlands, no.9 in Norway, no.12 in Austria and no.25 in the United States.

The success of *Kids In America*, while very welcome, also created problems within the Wilde family, especially for Ricky and Marty.

'The pressure was on,' said Kim. 'There was the expectation that we'd keep on churning out hit after hit. But we all share a passion for pop music, so we just went at it until we got it.'

Kids In America was remixed in 1993, for Kim's compilation album, *THE REMIX COLLECTION*. The remixed version was released as a single the following year in most countries, excluding the UK where its release was cancelled at the last minute, but it wasn't a hit.

Kim re-recorded *Kids In America* for her 2006 album, *NEVER SAY NEVER*, which again was passed over for release in the UK.

Kids In America was performed by Janet Jackson as Cleo Hewitt, with Billy Hufsey, Carlo Imperato, Gene Anthony Ray, Jesse Borrego, Nia Peeples & Valarie Landsburg, during Episode 14 – *The Heart Of Rock 'N' Roll II* – of Season 4 of the TV series *Fame*, which first aired on 26th January 1985 in the United States.

In 2006, *Kids In America* was sampled by the Scandinavian band Major Boys, on some remixes of their *Friday Night Boys* single, which were credited to Major Boys vs Kim Wilde. The single wasn't issued in the UK, but achieved no.11 in Finland.

2 ~ Chequered Love

UK: RAK RAK 330 (1981).
  B-side: *Shane*.

9.05.81: 32-9-**4-4**-5-18-26-44-56

Australia
17.08.81: peaked at no.**6**, charted for 21 weeks

Austria
1.09.81: **16**-18-17 (bi-weekly)

Belgium
27.06.81: 14-8-5-4-3-**2**-3-4-10-10-19-30

Denmark
10.07.81: 5-**3**-6-7-6-7-8-6-4-6-5-8-8-7-9-12-8-8-13

France
18.12.81: peaked at no.**64**, charted for 7 weeks

Germany
15.06.81: 50-13-8-5-3-3-3-3-**2**-6-5-5-9-11-12-18-19-21-33-31-48-47-65-65

Ireland
17.05.81: 13-6-**4-4**-8-13-30

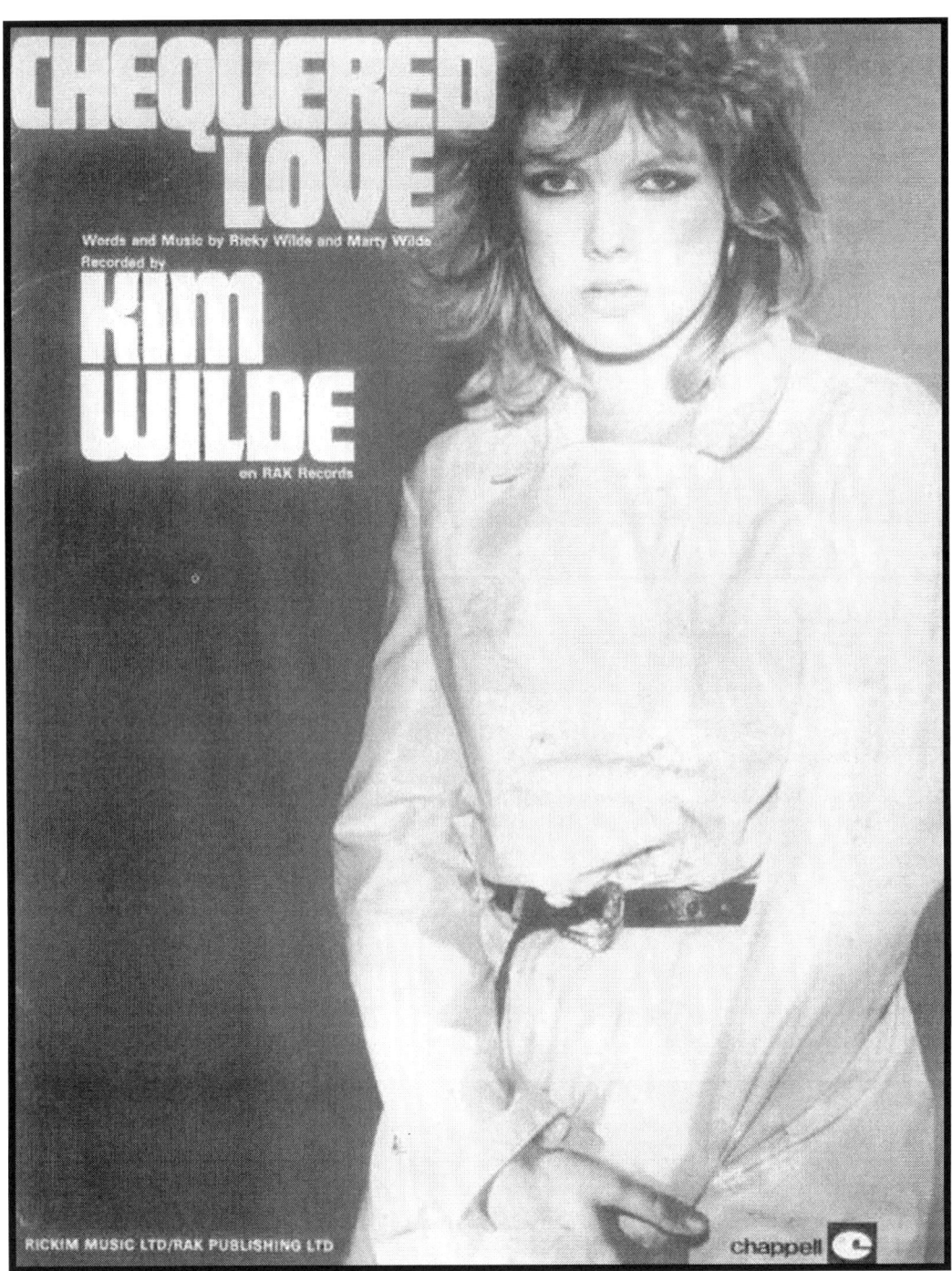

Netherlands
27.06.81: 11-3-3-**2**-5-6-6-8-39

South Africa
1.08.81: peaked at no.**1** (1), charted for 11 weeks

Sweden
3.07.81: 7-**6**-10-18 (bi-weekly)

Switzerland
12.07.81: 11-6-**2-2-2-2**-3-10-14

Zimbabwe
16.01.82: peaked at no.**6**, charted for 8 weeks

Like *Kids In America*, Kim's follow-up *Chequered Love* was written for her by her brother Ricky and her father Marty.

'I think it's a good pop song,' said Kim, 'it has a lot of energy. It's good fun, good entertainment and I enjoyed singing it – that's what it all boils down to.'

Chequered Love couldn't quite match the success of *Kids In America*, but nevertheless it was a sizeable hit, and gave Kim her second no.1 single in South Africa. Elsewhere, *Chequered Love* charted at no.2 in Belgium, Germany, the Netherlands and Switzerland, no.3 in Denmark, no.4 in Ireland and the UK, no.6 in Australia, Sweden and Zimbabwe, and no.16 in Austria.

3 ~ Water On Glass

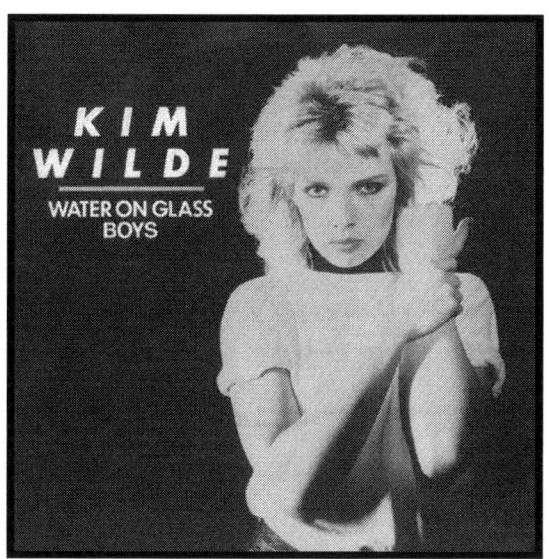

UK: RAK RAK 334 (1981).
  B-side: *Boys*.

1.08.81: 35-17-13-**11**-13-22-38-64 (*Water On Glass/Boys*)

Ireland
29.11.81: 13-**10-10**-20 (*Water On Glass*)

Water On Glass was composed by Ricky and Marty Wilde, and was recorded by Kim for her self-titled debut album. The track was only released as a single in the UK, Ireland and the Netherlands.

   Water On Glass charted at no.10 in Ireland and no.11 in the UK, where the non-album B-side *Boys* – another Ricky/Marty composition – was also listed.

4 ~ Cambodia

UK: RAK RAK 336 (1981).
  B-side: *Watching For Shapes*.

14.11.81: 45-32-24-18-**12**-15-17-17-19-39-43-68

Australia
14.12.81: peaked at no.**7**, charted for 24 weeks

Austria
1.02.82: 8-5-**4**-5-6-12-19 (bi-weekly)

Belgium
12.12.81: 30-26-26-24-13-12-7-5-**2**-3-6-8-8-12-19-23-29-39

Denmark
4.12.81: 6-**2-2-2-2-2**-4-5-5-4-5-5-4-5-4-3-3-**2**-4-6-9-12-13

Finland
12.81: peaked at no.**6**, charted for 12 weeks

France
5.02.82: peaked at no.**1** (14), charted for 34 weeks

Germany
23.11.81: 70-44-14-11-10-7-4-4-3-4-**2**-4-5-5-6-14-11-17-28-29-42-36-44-64-53-56

Ireland
29.11.81: 26-17-19-**15**-18-18-23-28

Netherlands
5.12.81: 47-45-33-35-34-27-13-7-8-**5**-9-8-9-9-14-27

New Zealand
7.03.82: **21**-42-39-x-x-43

Norway
12.12.81: 9-8-x-9-**3**-6-6-5-5-5-6-6-4-8-10

South Africa
16.01.82: peaked at no.**2**, charted for 16 weeks

Switzerland
20.12.81: 8-6-6-2-2-2-**1**-**1**-2-5-9-15

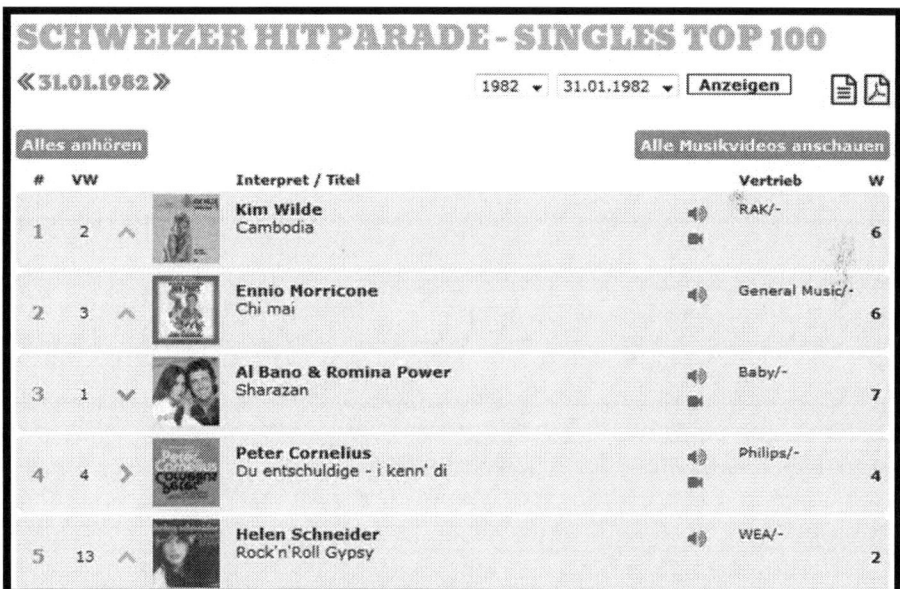

Zimbabwe
15.05.82: peaked at no.**18**, charted for 5 weeks

Sweden
8.12.81: 7-3-2-**1-1**-2-3-5-10-12-19 (bi-weekly)

#	LW	Artist / Title	Label / Company	Prefix / Suffix	W
1	2	Kim Wilde / Cambodia	RAK / EMI	006-6432	4
2	1	Attack / Ooa hela natten	CBS / CBS	CBS 1281	7
3	6	Kvack Kvack / Die Fogel-Song	Duck Records / Mariann	Kvack 1	7
4	4	Ebba Grön / Scheisse	Mislur / SAM-Distr.	MLR 24S	5
5	9	Rymdimperiet / Vod pojkar vill ha	Mistlur / SAM-Distr.	MLR 23S	3

Cambodia, like Kim's three previous singles, was written for her by her brother Ricky and her father Marty. Although Marty was interested in the South-East Asian conflict, the song wasn't intended to be political.

'It just sounds better than Birmingham,' said Kim. 'People hate that answer – it really pisses them off!'

The song itself is about a wife of an American pilot, who ends up being killed in the Cambodian conflict. 'The lyric was originally written in the first person,' said Kim, 'but while I could really identify with the woman in question, I have changed it, so that now I sing in the third person.'

Kim recorded *Cambodia* for her second album, *SELECT*, however, she felt it was so good a decision was taken to release as a single six months ahead of the album. The judgement was spot on, as Cambodia gave Kim a massive hit in continental Europe especially. The single version of the song was just under four minutes, while the full album version of the song was a lengthy 7:13 minutes long.

In France, *Cambodia* topped the chart for an impressive 14 weeks, and went on to sell over a million copies. The single also went to no.1 in Sweden and Switzerland, and achieved no.2 in Belgium, Denmark, Germany and South Africa, no.3 in Norway, no.4 in Austria, no.5 in the Netherlands, no.6 in Finland, no.7 in Australia, no.12 in the UK, no.15 in Ireland, no.18 in Zimbabwe and no.21 in New Zealand.

Cambodia has featured in two films, namely *Dans Paris* in 2006, and 2018's *The Stranger: Prey At Night*.

Marty Wilde recorded his own version of *Cambodia* for his 2020 album, *RUNNING TOGETHER*. The album also featured a duet with Kim, *60's World*.

5 ~ View From A Bridge

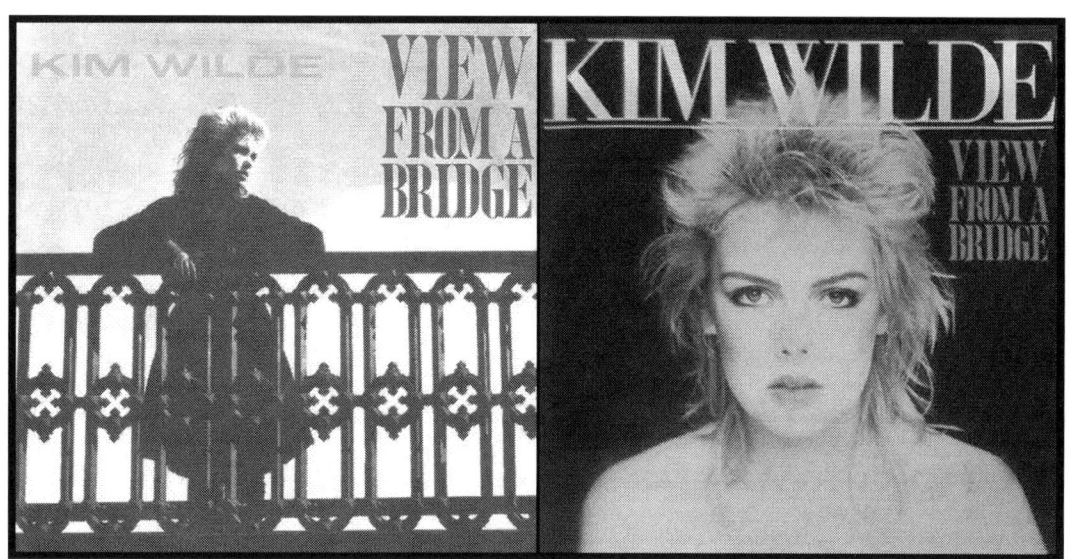

UK: RAK RAK 342 (1982).
  B-side: *Take Me Tonight*.

17.04.82: 44-30-18-**16**-25-32-66

Australia
17.05.82: peaked at no.**7**, charted for 20 weeks

Austria
15.05.82: 17-15-**10**-13-19-19 (bi-weekly)

Belgium
24.04.82: 22-9-5-5-5-**4**-6-20-27-39

Denmark
30.04.82: 6-5-**2-2-2**-6-7-7-9-11-x-12-12-11-12-11

Finland
04.82: peaked at no.**3**, charted for 12 weeks

France
30.07.82: peaked at no.**15**, charted for 22 weeks

Germany
19.04.82: 60-36-9-9-8-10-10-8-**6**-10-12-18-23-31-33-46-61-58-68

Ireland
2.05.82: 23-**16**-19-26

Netherlands
24.04.82: 8-**7**-**7**-8-11-15-24-37

Sweden
4.05.82: 5-5-**4**-5-8-x-x-20 (bi-weekly)

Switzerland
25.04.82: 15-9-**2**-**2**-**2**-**2**-3-4-6-11-15

Zimbabwe
17.07.82: peaked at no.**14**, charted for 6 weeks

Telling the tale of a girl who commits suicide by jumping from a bridge, after she discovers her lover with another girl, *View From A Bridge* was written by Ricky & Marty Wilde. Kim recorded the song for her second album, *SELECT*, and it was released as a single one month ahead of the album.

View From A Bridge continued Kim's impressive run of success, charting at no.2 in Denmark and Switzerland, no.3 in Finland, no.4 in Belgium and Sweden, no.6 in Germany, no.7 in Australia and the Netherlands, no.10 in Austria, no.14 in Zimbabwe, no.15 in France, and no.16 in Ireland and the UK.

Kim recorded a new, more uptempo dance version of *View From A Bridge* for her 2006 album, *NEVER SAY NEVER*.

6 ~ Child Come Away

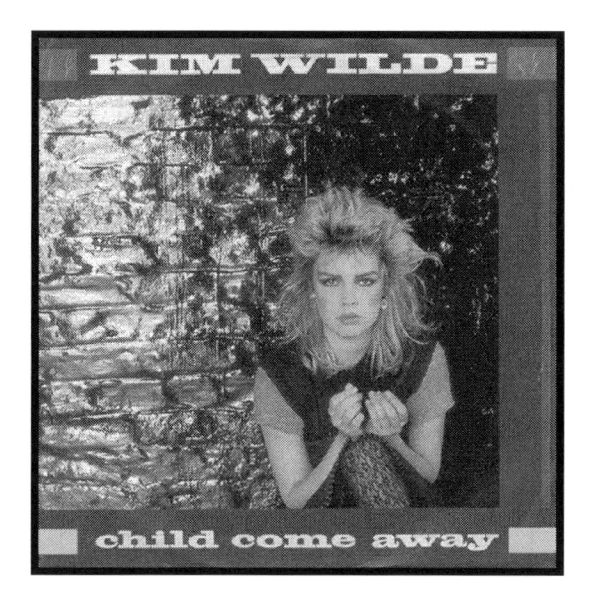

UK: RAK RAK 352 (1982).
  B-side: *Just Another Guy*.

16.10.82: 74-**43**-49-68

Australia
31.01.83: peaked at no.**76**, charted for 6 weeks

Belgium
20.11.82: 36-**25**-**25**-36

Denmark
29.10.82: 6-**4**-**4**-**4**-5

France
3.12.82: peaked at no.**21**, charted for 13 weeks

Germany
8.11.82: 37-40-37-63-51-69-53-62-**36**-44-68-66

Netherlands
6.11.82: **47**

Sweden
9.11.82: 15-18-12-**10** (bi-weekly)

Switzerland
21.11.82: 11-**6**-8-11-14

Child Come Away was written by Ricky & Marty Wilde, and was recorded by Kim as a non-album track.

Child Come Away was Kim's least successful single to date, and became her first to miss the Top 40 in the UK, where it peaked at no.43. The single fared better elsewhere, charting at no.4 in Denmark, no.6 in Switzerland, no.10 in Sweden, no.21 in France, no.25 in Belgium and no.36 in Germany.

KIM WILDE

NEW 7" & 12" SINGLE IN COLOUR PICTURE SLEEVE

LOVE BLONDE

c/w

CAN YOU HEAR IT

(12) RAK 360

12" INCLUDES SPECIAL LIMITED EDITION FREE POSTER
12 RAKS 360

RAK RECORDS

7 ~ Love Blonde

UK: RAK RAK 360 (1983).
B-side: *Can You Hear It*.

30.07.83: 41-34-24-**23-23**-27-38-56

Australia
19.09.83: peaked at no.**32**, charted for 14 weeks

Belgium
13.08.83: 25-15-12-8-**7**-9-12-28

Denmark
5.08.83: 8-5-**4-4-4**-10

Finland
08.83: peaked at no.**5**, charted for 12 weeks

France
27.08.83: peaked at no.**35**, charted for 23 weeks

Germany
22.08.83: 44-54-37-27-**26**-30-27-38-42-36-58-62-68-63-65

Ireland
14.08.83: **29**

Netherlands
6.08.83: 37-19-**13**-21-21-30-33-39

Sweden
9.08.83: 10-**7**-11-11 (bi-weekly)

Switzerland
14.08.83: 14-12-**11**

Love Blonde was written by Ricky & Marty Wilde, and it is a song Kim was initially reluctant to record.

'I had kind of a problem with that at the time,' she admitted. 'Should I really be singing this song about me? And I asked Dad, "Is it about me?" And he said, "No, it's about the mythology of the blonde sex symbol".'

Kim pointed out that's exactly how she was perceived by everyone.

'He told me to just take the piss out of it and enjoy it,' she said. 'Most people have fun playing about with my image, talking about me, so I thought, "Why not do it myself?".'

Kim recorded *Love Blonde* for her 1983 album, *CATCH AS CATCH CAN*, and it was released as the album's lead single. In most countries it proved more successful than Kim's previous single, *Child Come Away*, and achieved no.4 in Denmark, no.5 in Finland, no.7 in Belgium and Sweden, no.11 in Switzerland, no.13 in the Netherlands, no.23 in the UK, no.26 in Germany, no.29 in Ireland, no.32 in Australia and no.35 in France.

Kim promoted *Love Blonde* with a music video in which she made a conscious effort to change her image.

'When I watch *Beat It* or *Billie Jean*,' she said, 'I can't wait to see Michael Jackson appear, see him move, dance. So in my clips, I decided to show off my sex appeal … in *Love Blonde*, I had this sexy black dress and I thought it changed from the usual rock uniform. That's why I don't like the clip of *Cambodia* – it's too commonplace.'

November 19, 1983   45p

Biggest ever issue!

KING KURT - UP WITH SKIRTS!

record
mirror

BLONDES HAVE MORE FUNK
Kim Wilde, page 32

8 ~ Dancing In The Dark

UK: RAK RAK 365 (1983).
 B-side: *Back Seat Driver*.

12.11.83: **67**-74

Belgium
19.11.83: 31-**11**-17-28

Denmark
25.11.83: 15-6-5-6-**4**-**4**-6-5-6-6-8-15

Finland
12.83: peaked at no.**8**, charted for 8 weeks

Germany
21.11.83: 65-x-**26**-32-27-34-31-36-32-38-48-55-66

Switzerland
4.12.83: 19-17-11-12-**9**-11-11-19-23

Dancing In The Dark was written by Nicky Chinn and Paul Gurvitz, and was recorded by Kim for her 1983 album, *CATCH AS CATCH CAN*. When it was released as the follow-up to *Love Blonde*, it became Kim's first single not composed by her brother Ricky and father Marty.

'Dad and Ricky wrote and produced some very big hits for me,' said Kim. 'That doesn't mean that I don't try out some work from other from time to time as well. They do a lot of work for the album, but they have to write hits too, of course.'

Dancing In the Dark charted at no.4 in Denmark, no.8 in Finland, no.9 in Switzerland, no.11 in Belgium and no.26 in Germany.

In the UK, however, *Dancing In The Dark* struggled and could only manage two weeks in the Top 75, peaking at a lowly no.67.

Kim later admitted she wasn't happy with the song.

'No-one expected that *Dancing In The Dark* would do so badly,' she said. 'Every Monday I woke up in fear, and asked my record company if the record had made the charts yet. They reacted coldly.'

Kim felt she had disappointed everyone, and as a result her self-confidence suffered.

'After *Dancing In The Dark*,' she said, 'I thought "I can't carry on much longer like this – I've got to get my song writing together". Not just because the single was a flop, but because I wasn't happy with it as a song, and I wasn't happy wasting my time promoting it when I could be song writing.'

Dancing In The Dark proved to be the last single Kim released on the RAK record label in the UK.

9 ~ House Of Salome

UK: Not Released.

Netherlands: EMI 1A 006-2001987 (1983).
  B-side: *Sing It Out For Love*.

Belgium
7.07.84: **36-36**

House Of Salome was written by Ricky & Marty Wilde, and was recorded by Kim for her *CATCH AS CATCH CAN* album.
   The track was issued as the third single from the album in a small number of countries, including France, Germany, Netherlands, Spain and South Africa. It was the first of Kim's singles to not be released in the UK.
   The only country where *House Of Salome* charted is Belgium, where it spent two weeks at no.36, before dropping off the chart again.

OK!

âge tendre — 4 F seulement

DES MAGAZINES DE JEUNES

DE MISS OK ! POUR SOIGNER VOTRE FORME PAR LE SPORT

PATRICK SEBASTIEN A EMMENÉ SON... ILS EN TOURNÉE

MODE EN AVANT-PREMIÈRE

LES TENDANCES DE LA RENTRÉE

UNE CONFESSION EXCLUSIVE KIM WILDE : « J'AIME SURTOUT LES HOMMES PETITS »

HOROSCOPE : SPÉCIAL VIERGE

LES PREMIÈRES IMAGES DU NOUVEAU CLIP DE TÉLÉPHONE

M 2272 - 449 - 4,00 F

10 ~ The Second Time

UK: MCA Records KIM 1 (1984).
B-side: *Lovers On A Beach*.

13.10.84: 52-33-**29-29**-37-59

Belgium
20.10.84: 36-28-28-**15**-16-39

Denmark
2.11.84: 15-12-12-10-x-14-**8-8**-11-11

Germany
22.10.84: 69-17-16-11-11-**9**-12-13-15-23-26-38-41-54-72

Netherlands
20.10.84: 27-31-**23**-29-37-39

Switzerland
28.10.84: 27-18-16-11-11-**7**-11-13-17-19-25-29

USA
19.01.85: 82-75-68-**65**-70-80-97 (as *Go For It*)

The Second Time was written by Kim's brother, now credited as Ricki rather than Ricky, and her father Marty. Kim recorded the song for her 1984 album, *TEASES & DARES*. The album was recorded at the Wilde family's new Select Sound Studios in Knebworth, North Hertfordshire, England, and was Kim's first for her new record label, MCA, after her contract with RAK expired.

Kim decided to leave RAK 'Just because the contract that binds us had come to an end, and let's say we had done everything we could do together. That was the best thing to do.'

The Second Time returned Kim to the Top 40 in the UK, where it peaked at no.29. The single also achieved no.7 in Switzerland, no.8 in Demark, no.9 in Germany, no.15 in Belgium and no.23 in the Netherlands.

The Second Time was issued as a 7" picture disc single in the UK only.

'I'm happy with it,' said Kim, 'it's a strong single … there's a hidden reference to the second coming of my career, but the lyric has multiple meanings.'

In North America, *The Second Time* was re-titled *Go For It*, and it gave Kim only her second entry on the Hot 100 in the United States after *Kids In America*, peaking at no.65.

KIM WILDE

NEW SINGLE
THE TOUCH
AVAILABLE ON 7" & 12"

TAKEN FROM HER HIT ALBUM
TEASES & DARES

MCA RECORDS
72-78 Brewer Street London W1

11 ~ The Touch

UK: MCA Records KIM 2 (1984).
  B-side: *Shangri-La*.

8.12.84: 63-**56**-65

Belgium
26.01.85: 35-34-22-22-**20**-32

Germany
4.02.85: 45-38-**29**-34-35-43-53-65-70-x-75

Netherlands
26.01.85: 45-**34**-35-35-43

The Touch was written by Ricki & Marty Wilde, and was recorded by Kim for her *TEASES & DARES* album.
   Chosen as the album's second single, *The Touch* failed to match the success of *The Second Time*, and didn't sell well enough to chart in many countries. *The Touch* did achieve no.20 in Belgium, no.29 in Germany and no.34 in the Netherlands.

In the UK, despite a shaped 7" picture disc being released, *The Touch* peaked at a disappointing no.56 during a brief, three week chart run.

12 ~ Rage To Love

UK: MCA Records KIM 3 (1985).
  B-side: *Putty In Your Hands*.

27.04.85: 54-38-29-22-**19**-26-41-62

Australia
27.05.85: peaked at no.**94**, charted for 2 weeks

Germany
22.04.85: 60-64-**45**-46-53-71

Rage To Love was written by Ricki & Marty Wilde, and was recorded by Kim for her *TEASES & DARES* album.

'I think *Rage To Love* was a brilliant record,' said Kim. 'We got Dave Edmunds to remix that, and it sounded very Stray Cats-ish.'

Released as the third and final single from *TEASES & DARES*, *Rage To Love* was issued as a 7" shaped picture disc in the UK, where it gave Kim her biggest hit for three years, rising to no.19.

Elsewhere, however, *Rage To Love* was much less successful, only achieving no.45 in Germany and a lowly no.94 in Australia.

13 ~ Schoolgirl

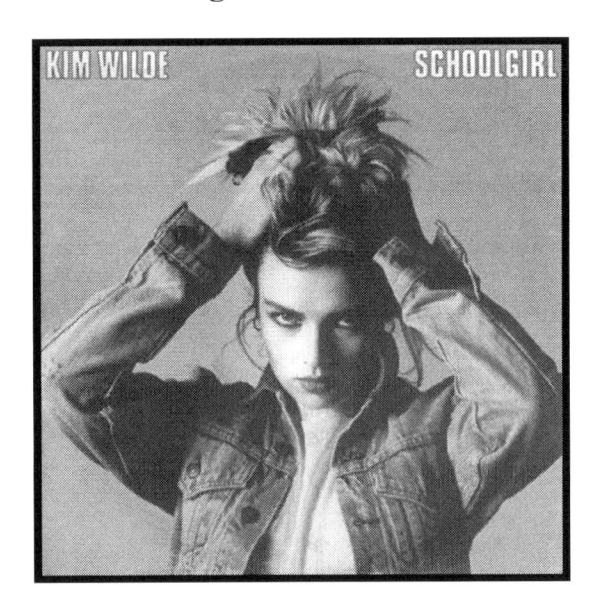

UK: Not Released.

Europe: MCA Records 258 650-7 (1986).
  B-side: *Songs About Love*.

Denmark
4.07.86: 14-6-**5-5**-7-7

Germany
21.07.86: **38**-46-**38**-55-57-74

Netherlands
12.07.86: 47-**36**-49

Inspired by Kim's younger sister Roxanne, *Schoolgirl* was the first Top 40 success Kim co-wrote herself, along with Ricki & Marty Wilde.
  'The single is dedicated to my sister,' Kim confirmed. 'My brother and my father, Ricky and Marty, have written the music. I wanted to write the lyrics and the vocal melody. I wanted to speak to my sister, but also to other young people and their problems – but the bottom line is that the song is optimistic.'
  Kim recorded *Schoolgirl* for her 1988 album, *ANOTHER STEP*, and it was released as a single in Australia and several continental European countries.
  Schoolgirl achieved no.5 in Denmark, no.36 in the Netherlands and no.38 in Germany.
  Songs About Love, the non-album B-side of *Schoolgirl*, was a song solely written and produced by Kim.

14 ~ You Keep Me Hangin' On

UK: MCA Records KIM 4 (1986).
B-side: *Loving You*.

25.10.86: 36-15-6-**2**-**2**-3-7-15-22-28-26-26-42-60

Pos	LW	Title, Artist		Peak Pos	WoC
1	1	TAKE MY BREATH AWAY (LOVE THEME FROM 'TOP GUN') BERLIN	CBS	1	4
2	6 ↑	YOU KEEP ME HANGIN' ON KIM WILDE	MCA	2	4
3	4 ↑	WALK LIKE AN EGYPTIAN THE BANGLES	CBS	3	10
4	8 ↑	SHOWING OUT (GET FRESH AT THE WEEKEND) MEL AND KIM	SUPREME	4	9
5	17 ↑	BREAKOUT SWING OUT SISTER	MERCURY	5	5

Australia
1.12.86: peaked at no.**1** (2), charted for 28 weeks

Austria
15.02.87: 27-**20**-22-24-30 (bi-weekly)

ORIGINAL SHEET MUSIC EDITION
YOU KEEP ME
HANGIN' ON
Recorded by Kim Wilde on MCA Records
ords and Music by Eddie Holland, Lamont Dozier, and Brian Holland
ORKNEY IS.
Aberdeen
Edinburgh
Liverpool
Hull
Manchester
Birmingham
THE NETHERLANDS
Amsterdam
London
Brussels
Versailles
Paris
Orléans
FRANCE
JOBETE
JOBETE MUSIC CO., INC.
KIM WILDE

Belgium
25.10.86: 39-27-30
31.01.87: 30-**16**-18-31

Denmark
3.10.86: 11-**3**-5-5-4-9-11-12

France
6.12.86: 43-47-46-32-28-22-23-20-23-25-**19**-27-24-31-29-46-47

Germany
22.12.86: 24-13-15-**8**-12-13-16-25-37-46-59-70-72

Ireland
2.11.86: 12-7-**2-2**-7-x-x-x-x-30-29

Japan
28.11.86: peaked at no.**75**, charted for 5 weeks

Netherlands
27.12.86: 33-19-21-**17**-18-21-23-36-56-63-89

New Zealand
21.12.86: 39-39-39-39-39-40-33-35-25-14-17-17-27-15-14-**12**-31-28-37-37

Norway
17.01.87: 8-5-3-**1-1-1**-2-2-3-5

#	LW		Artist Title	W
1	3	^	Kim Wilde — You Keep Me Hangin' On	4
2	1	v	Bon Jovi — Livin' On A Prayer	8
3	2	v	Red Box — For America	10
4	5	^	The Housemartins — Caravan Of Love	3
5	7	^	Gary Moore — Over The Hills And Far Away	3

VG Lista - Singles Top 20 — 06/1987

Switzerland
4.01.87: 5-3-3-**2**-4-4-10-17-18-25

USA
28.03.87: 96-70-51-39-29-23-14-8-4-2-**1**-2-8-17-30-39-48-63-80-85-96

You Keep Me Hangin' On was composed by Holland-Dozier-Holland, and was originally recorded by the Supremes for their 1967 album, *THE SUPREMES SING HOLLAND-DOZIER-HOLLAND*.

The Supremes took *You Keep Me Hangin' On* to no.1 on the Hot 100 in the United States, and to no.8 in the UK.

Kim, unusually for her, recorded a cover of *You Keep Me Hangin' On* for her *ANOTHER STEP* album.

'Ricky was playing with some chord changes,' she said, 'and realised they weren't his, they were from *You Keep Me Hangin' On*. He wasn't sure whether to continue writing an original song with the chords, or to do the cover, but he ended up doing the cover.'

Ricky's work was then forgotten, until someone reminded him and Kim about it.

'I wasn't keen on doing a cover originally,' Kim admitted, 'It was my brother's idea to record the song. I hadn't actually heard the original song for ages when I went into the studio, and I made a point of not listening to it until I'd recorded it because I wanted to inject some originality into it.'

Kim liked the fact the song had heart, and was emotional. 'I like songs about emotion,' she said. 'I've always been influenced by Stevie Wonder and Aretha Franklin. America's just got so much to offer musically, it's great.'

'So I went in and did this throwaway vocal,' said Kim. 'I liked the way we'd done it, and the fact that it was a totally original approach to the song.'

Kim and Ricky decided to treat *You Keep Me Hangin' On* as a new song, even tweaking the lyrics in parts, and Kim was rewarded with the biggest hit of her career in many countries.

In the United States, *You Keep Me Hangin' On* went all the way to no.1 on the Hot 100. The single also hit no.1 in Australia and Norway, but Kim had to settle for two weeks at no.2 in the UK, behind Berlin's *You Take My Breathe Away*.

Elsewhere, *You Keep Me Hangin' On* achieved no.2 in Ireland and Switzerland, no.3 in Denmark, no.8 in Germany, no.12 in New Zealand, no.16 in Belgium, no.17 in the Netherlands, no.19 in France and no.20 in Austria.

Kim was chuffed, when the song's co-writer Lamont Dozier sent her a telegram, saying how much he liked her version of his song.

LET IT BE

UK: The Sun AID 1 (1987).
 B-side: *Let It Be (The Gospel Jam Mix)*.

4.04.87: **1-1-1**-4-17-34-58

Pos	LW	Title, Artist		Peak Pos	WoC
1	New	LET IT BE FERRY AID	THE SUN	1	1
2	1 ↓	RESPECTABLE MEL AND KIM	SUPREME	1	5
3	9 ↑	LET'S WAIT A WHILE JANET JACKSON	BREAKOUT	3	3
4	4	WITH OR WITHOUT YOU U2	ISLAND	4	2
5	New	LA ISLA BONITA MADONNA	SIRE	5	1

Austria
15.05.87: 10-**4**-9-16-20-22-25 (bi-weekly)

Belgium
18.04.87: 18-8-**3**-4-6-8-12-24-38

France
25.04.87: 35-37-32-23-19-14-**8**-11-13-13-19-20-24-34-34

Germany
20.04.87: 47-8-5-4-4-**3**-7-9-12-14-29-39-47-63

Ireland
29.03.87: 22-**2-2**-3-7-21

Netherlands
11.04.87: 21-7-**4-4-4**-7-7-11-20-45-46-49-88

New Zealand
7.06.87: 22-16-11-**4**-11-23-38-47

Norway
18.04.87: 4-4-**1-1-1-1**-2-2-2-5-6

#	LW		Artist / Title	W
1	4	^	**Ferry Aid** Let It Be	3
2	2	>	**Mel & Kim** Respectable	5
3	3	>	**Starship** Nothing's Gonna Stop Us Now	6
4	6	^	**Mental As Anything** Live It Up	4
5	1	v	**Boy George** Everything I Own	6

VG Lista - Singles Top 20 — 1987, 18/1987

Sweden
6.05.87: 10-**9-9**-16-18

Switzerland
26.04.87: 3-**1-1-1-1**-2-1-3-3-8-11-11-25-19

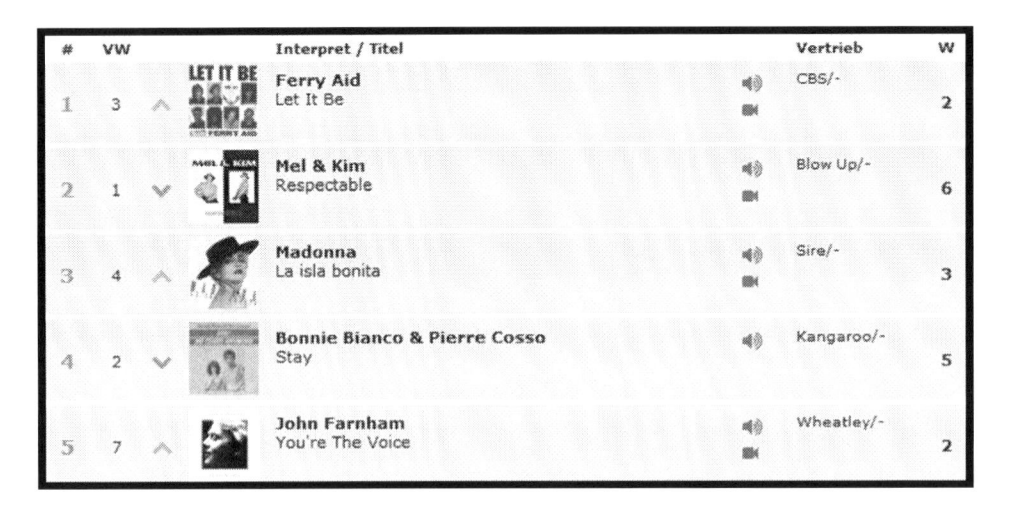

#	VW		Interpret / Titel		Vertrieb	W
1	3	∧	**Ferry Aid** Let It Be		CBS/-	2
2	1	∨	**Mel & Kim** Respectable		Blow Up/-	6
3	4	∧	**Madonna** La isla bonita		Sire/-	3
4	2	∨	**Bonnie Bianco & Pierre Cosso** Stay		Kangaroo/-	5
5	7	∧	**John Farnham** You're The Voice		Wheatley/-	2

Let It Be was written by John Lennon & Paul McCartney, and was originally recorded by The Beatles for their 1970 album with the same title. The Beatles took the song to no.1 in Australia, Austria, Canada, The Netherlands, New Zealand, Norway, Switzerland and the USA, no.2 in Germany and the UK, and no.3 in Belgium and Ireland.

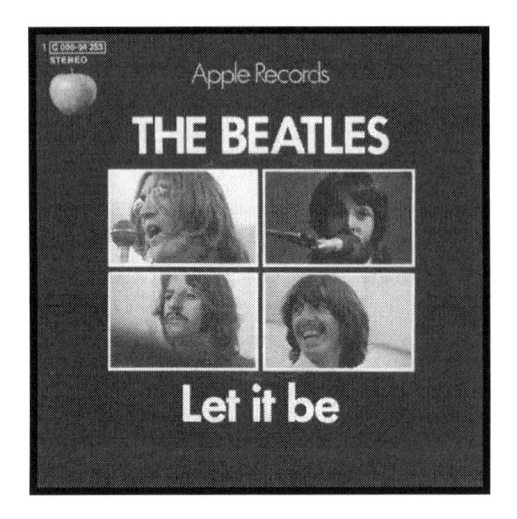

On 6th March 1987, in the Belgium port of Zeebrugge, the ferry *MS Herald of Free Enterprise* capsized and sank, with the loss of 193 passengers and crew. In response to the Zeebrugge Disaster Garry Bushell, who worked for *The Sun* newspaper at the time, organised a charity recording of *Let It Be*, which took place between the 15th and 17th March. The recording was credited to Ferry Aid.

Somewhat reluctantly, Kim was one of the numerous artists who contributed to the recording. 'I didn't think, when I heard, that this was a good thing to do,' she said.

'Making a record wasn't the first thing that sprang to mind. I was very upset by what happened and I didn't think it was appropriate to sing about it. I'm doing it because I've been told the families need the money, but I feel very strange about it.'

Kim, with Nik Kershaw, was one of the solo vocalists on the recording. Among the others were Paul McCartney, Andy Bell, Boy George, Edwin Starr, Jackie Graham, Kate Bush, Mel and Kim, Pepsi & Shirley and Ruby Turner. Gary Moore and Mark Knopfler performed the guitar solo.

The chorus featured a host of other artists, including Alvin Stardust, Bananarama, Bonnie Tyler, Bucks Fizz, The Drifters, Errol Brown, Frankie Goes To Hollywood, Go West, Hazel Dean, Imagination, Loose Ends, Maxi Priest, New Seekers, The Nolans and Suzi Quatro.

Ferry Aid's cover of *Let It Be* topped the charts in Norway, Switzerland and the UK, and achieved no.2 in Ireland, no.3 in Belgium and Germany, no.4 in Austria, the Netherlands and New Zealand, no.8 in France and no.9 in Sweden.

15 ~ Another Step (Closer To You)

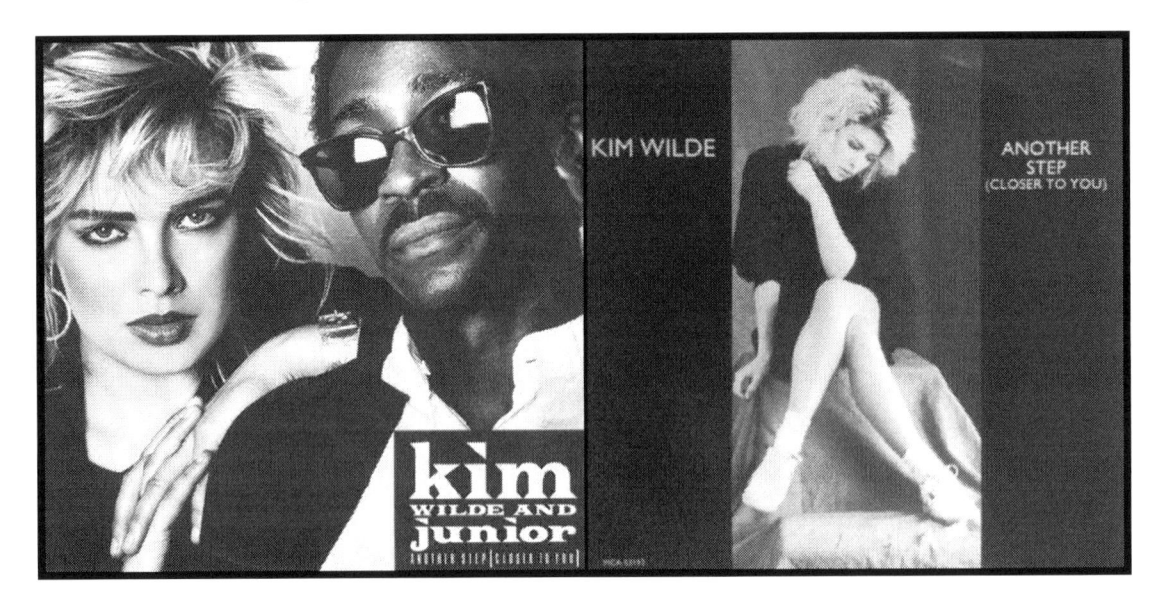

UK: MCA Records KIM 5 (1987).
  B-side: *Hold Back*.

4.04.87: 52-32-20-14-9-9-**6**-8-17-26-54

Australia
27.04.87: peaked at no.**88**, charted for 5 weeks

Ireland
12.04.87: 28-24-9-**6**-10-12-15-22

Netherlands
16.05.87: **95**

Kim co-wrote *Another Step (Closer To You)* with Steve Byrd, and the two of them recorded a demo of the song as a duet. However, agreeing the track really needed a more soulful male vocal, Kim recorded the song with Junior Giscombe for her *ANOTHER STEP* album.
　'It was just a matter of finding someone to sing the song,' said Kim, 'and his (Junior's) name came up in conversation, and I went "Yeah", and so it was spontaneous, like all duets should be.'
　'Kim just rang and said "Are you up for it?",' said Junior, 'and I said "Yeah, great" 'cos it gave me a chance to go out or whatever. I was chuffed at the fact they thought it was good enough to be a single, and the next thing you know I'm back on TV and stuff.'

Kim readily admitted when she first started out, she didn't have the confidence to even think about writing songs.

'I never thought it was a move I could make,' she said, 'composing myself. I lacked self-confidence. But when you sit down, feel depressed, often you discover there is a way out and I discovered I like to sit and fiddle with melodies. In the beginning, I hadn't the feeling that they would end up on the record.'

Once she started writing for herself, Kim felt her career started to make a lot more sense.

'That's when it felt more like a proper career,' she said. 'I didn't feel so much like an imposter.'

In most countries, *Another Step (Closer To You)* was issued as the follow-up to *You Keep Me Hangin' On*. Before releasing the song as a single, Ricky not only remixed the track, he also re-recorded most of it, although he did retain the original vocals.

Another Step (Closer To You) achieved no.6 in both Ireland and the UK, but it was only a minor hit in Australia and the Netherlands, and failed to chart at all in most countries.

16 ~ Say You Really Want Me

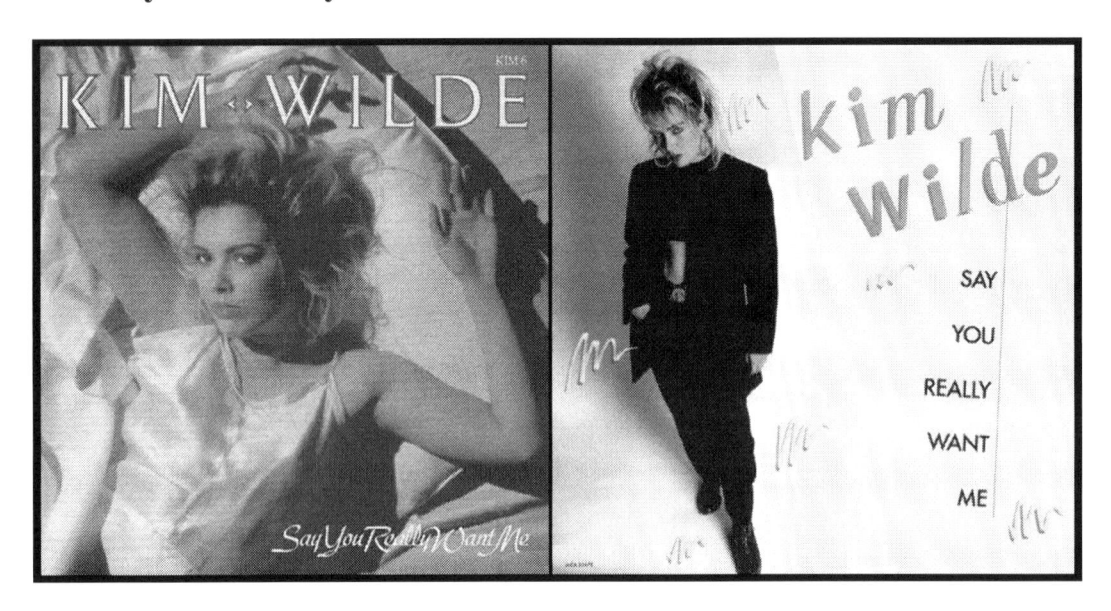

UK: MCA Records KIM 6 (1987).
   B-side: *Don't Say Nothing's Changed*.

8.08.87: 48-33-**29**-32-46

Ireland
16.08.87: 20-**18**

USA
18.07.87: 89-73-65-55-**44**-53-69-97

Say You Really Want Me was written by Danny Sembello, Dick Rudolf and Donnell Spencer, Jr., and was originally recorded by Kim for the soundtrack of the 1986 film, *Running Scared*, an action comedy that starred Gregory Hines and Billy Crystal.
   'Suddenly I got a phone call from top producer Rod Temperton,' said Kim. 'He needed a singer for a disco song for the movie, and the boss of my American record company suggested me. So I flew to L.A. … I was surprised to get the opportunity because the song is so good, that the biggest American singer would have recorded it.'

Say You Really Want Me was released as a single in North America only in 1986 but, despite Kim hoping for a big hit, it failed to chart.

An edited version of the song later featured on Kim's 1986 album, ANOTHER STEP. Following the success of *You Keep Me Hangin' On*, the single was re-released, and this time it did enter the Hot 100 in the United States, rising to no.44.

Say You Really Want Me was also issued as a single in Australia, Ireland and the UK, and it charted at no.18 in Ireland and no.29 in the UK.

NUMBER ONE
ONLY 45p

1987

IT'S **MEL** AND **KIM!**

BUMPER CHRISTMAS ISSUE!!!

EH? WHAT DO YOU MEAN WE'RE A MONTH TOO EARLY?

COMMUNARDS FREDDIE MERCURY JANET JACKSON'S SUPERFAN ERIC B'S WARDROBE AND LOADS OF TINSEL MISTLETOE MINCE PIES STOCKINGS HOLLY AND CHRISTMAS FAIRIES...

17 ~ Rockin' Around The Christmas Tree

UK: 10 Records TEN 2 (1987).
  B-side: *Deck The Blooming Halls* (The Mel Smith Yuletide Choir).

5.12.87: 39-13-6-**3**-**3**-10-31
24.12.88: 99

Denmark
15.12.17: 36-32-32-27
7.12.18: 24-30-33-22
6.12.19: 30-26-18-**16**

Ireland
13.12.87: 10-5-**4**-**4**-14
18.12.88: 19-20-20

Norway
26.12.87: **9-9**

Rockin' Around The Christmas Tree was composed by Johnny Marks, and was originally recorded by Brenda Lee in 1958, when she was just 13 years old.
  'I was only twelve *(sic)*, and I had not a lot of success in records,' said Brenda Lee, 'but for some reason he (Johnny Marks) wanted me to do it, and I did.'
  Although it was released as a single in both 1958 and 1959, it wasn't until 1960 that *Rockin' Around The Christmas Tree* finally entered the Hot 100 in the United States,

peaking at no.14. Thank to streaming, the song now re-enters the chart regularly during the festive season, and rose as high as no.2 in 2019.

Rockin' Around The Christmas Tree didn't enter the UK chart until 1962, when it peaked at no.6. More recently, the song has risen as high as no.9 in 2017, largely thanks to streaming.

Kim recorded a cover of *Rockin' Around The Christmas Tree* with Mel Smith, as Mel & Kim, for Comic Relief. Everyone involved with the single gave their time free, with the proceeds going to Oxfam and Save The Children, for their work in Ethiopia and Sudan, and UK-based alcohol and drug abuse, disability and homeless charities.

'The real Mel and Kim helped us a little with the record,' said Mel Smith.

'We sent them a rough demo version of the song from day one,' said Kim, 'and they were right behind it. I think they saw the joke.'

The duo promoted the song with a humorous video featuring Mel Smith's comedy partner, Griff Rhys Jones, plus Curiosity Killed The Cat and Spitting Images puppets of Tina Turner and Bette Midler. However, after the first screening, the BBC banned the original version of the video as it featured a clip of Kim opening a fridge to find Mel hiding inside.

'We had a number of calls claiming we were irresponsible,' said a BBC spokeswoman, 'because the shot encourages youngsters to climb into a fridge – with dangerous consequences.'

The video was duly re-edited, with Mel now shown sitting in a fridge cut-out instead.

'I think they have over-reacted,' said Kim, 'but you can never be too careful where children are concerned. They do copy their favourite stars and it could be very dangerous. It was an oversight but obviously no harm was meant.'

Kim's version of *Rockin' Around The Christmas Tree* charted at no.3 in the UK, no.4 in Ireland and no.9 in Norway – however, in the streaming age, it tends to be largely overlooked, thanks to the popularity of Brenda Lee's original recording. The only country where Kim's version has charted in recent years is Denmark, where it rose to no.27 in 2017, no.22 in 2018 and no.16 in 2019.

Kim re-recorded *Rockin' Around The Christmas Tree* with Nik Kershaw, for her 2013 festive album, *WILDE WINTER SONGBOOK*. The album was a very minor no.169 hit in the UK, but to date it is Kim's only studio album not to achieve Top 40 status anywhere.

18 ~ Hey Mister Heartache

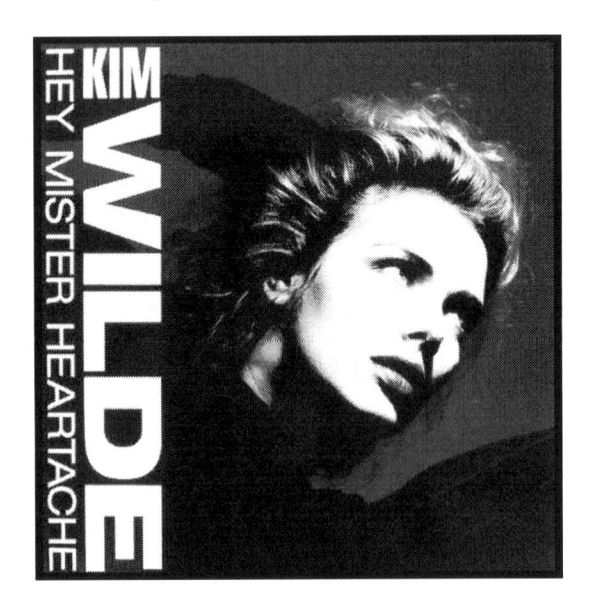

UK: MCA Records KIM 7 (1988).
 B-side: *Tell Me Where You Are*.

14.05.88: 51-38-**31**-38-62

Australia
4.07.88: **96**

Denmark
27.05.88: 10-8-**4**-5-6-8-10-13

Germany
16.05.88: 22-18-15-**13**-17-15-19-19-29-41-35-63-64-75

Ireland
22.05.88: 27-**22**

Italy
11.06.88: peaked at no.**8**, charted for 16 weeks

Netherlands
14.05.88: 70-53-36-36-**35**-46-52-66-69-72

Norway
7.05.88: 9-9-8-**3**-**3**-8-5-4-4-6-9

Switzerland
22.05.88: 14-20-16-**12**-13-17-13-14-17-21-24-x-30

Kim co-wrote *Hey Mister Heartache* with Steve Byrd, and she recorded the songs for her 1988 album, *CLOSE*.

The album version of the song featured uncredited vocals by Junior Giscombe, however, these were largely edited from the single version when *Hey Mister Heartache* was released as the album's lead single.

Hey Mister Heartache charted at no.3 in Norway, no.4 in Denmark, no.8 in Italy, no.12 in Switzerland, no.13 in Germany, no.22 in Ireland, no.31 in the UK and no.35 in the Netherlands.

19 ~ You Came

UK: MCA Records KIM 8 (1988).
  B-side: *Stone*.

16.07.88: 38-16-6-4-**3**-4-8-13-22-34-50

Australia
12.09.88: peaked at no.**31**, charted for 21 weeks

Austria
1.10.88: 13-**8**-12-18-18-24-16-28 (bi-weekly)
1.09.06: 33-30-29-24-25-30-31-49-48-50-59-73-72-75 (2006)

Belgium
27.08.88: 38-31-30-22-**10-10-10**-13-16-20-26
9.09.06: 45-49-x-40-33-43

Denmark
5.08.88: 4-4-4-2-**1-1-1-1**-2-3-5-7-11-12-11

Finland
07.88: peaked at no.**5**, charted for 12 weeks

France
25.06.88: 47-25-22-18-25-21-19-22-9-9-9-**5**-7-9-**5**-7-9-7-14-12-12-12-32

YOU CAME

Words and Music by KIM WILDE and RICKY WILDE
Recorded on MCA Records by

KIM WILDE

Germany
1.08.88: 42-16-10-7-**5-5**-6-**5**-6-7-11-15-27-41-50-52-67
1.09.06: 20-26-23-26-38-38-47-51-64 (2006)

Ireland
24.07.88: 15-9-4-**3**-5-8-16-27

Italy
17.09.88: peaked at no.**3**, charted for 24 weeks

Netherlands
6.08.88: 90-82-60-41-36-25-19-12-**11-11**-18-21-31-56-63-93
16.09.06: 50-45-33-30-34-49-39-51-68-83 (2006)

Norway
13.08.88: 10-9-**4**-6-5-9-6-5-8-10

Sweden
7.09.88: 12-9-**7**-9-12-17 (bi-weekly)
28.09.06: 38-25-43-55 (2006)

Switzerland
21.08.88: 18-4-4-4-**3**-5-5-4-7-17-16-22-29-21
3.09.06: 19-22-34-40-34-41-45-53-58-53-70-97-98 (2006)

USA
17.09.88: 84-73-59-50-46-**41**-42-57-77-90

Kim co-wrote *You Came* with her brother Ricky, and she recorded the song for her 1988 album, *CLOSE* – it was one of the last songs written for the album.

'My brother Ricky wrote the music,' said Kim. 'He told me he'd been inspired to write the music because he's just had a son, so that in turn inspired me to write the lyrics. I mean, he came into all our lives, and children have this way of becoming the most important thing in your lives.'

You Came was released as the follow-up to *Hey Mister Heartache* in the summer of 1988, when Kim was supporting Michael Jackson on the European leg of his hugely successful Bad Tour. It was, Kim admits, a surreal experience.

'I was thrown into the thick of it and it was a sink or swim situation,' she said. 'I was on tour with someone who was perceived as the greatest artist of that generation and it was pretty overwhelming for me. But I really managed to step up and it was one of the best things to happen to my career at the time.'

Although she played over 30 dates with him, Kim met Michael Jackson only once, for publicity shots to be taken. However, on stage and backstage footage from the Bad Tour featured in Kim's promo video for *You Came*.

'I really won't hear a bad word said about him (Michael Jackson),' said Kim. 'The adverse press I read about him I find personally very repulsive. All I can say is that the person I met was very sane, very normal, very sweet and very lovely. He had a gorgeous smile, and you can tell a lot about a person by the way they smile.'

You Came gave Kim one of the biggest hits of her career in many countries. The single hit no.1 in Denmark, and achieved no.3 in Ireland, Italy, Switzerland and the UK, no.4 in Norway, no.5 in Finland, France and Germany, no.7 in Sweden, no.8 in Austria, no.10 in Belgium, no.11 in the Netherlands, no.31 in Australia and no.41 in the United States.

Kim re-recorded *You Came* for her 2006 album, *NEVER SAY NEVER*, which wasn't released in the UK. In countries where the album was released, the new version of *You Came* was released as a single, to promote the album.

The 2006 version of *You Came* charted at no.19 in Switzerland, no.20 in Germany, no.24 in Austria, no.25 in Sweden, no.30 in the Netherlands and no.33 in Belgium.

20 ~ Never Trust A Stranger

UK: MCA Records KIM 9 (1988).
 B-side: *Wotcha Gonna Do*.

1.10.88: 50-32-15-**7**-9-13-20-23-43

Austria
15.01.89: 14-8-11-**7**-25-29 (bi-weekly)

Belgium
12.11.88: 29-28-27-18-18-13-9-7-**6-6**-7-12-16-27

Denmark
21.10.88: 11-5-**2-2**-4-3-5-8-7-8-8-14-14

Finland
11.88: peaked at no.**3**, charted for 8 weeks

France
10.12.88: 28-29-27-22-24-24-23-23-**20**-26-25-32-30-34

Germany
24.10.88: 74-29-18-12-**11**-12-17-18-20-29-34-39-47-62-74

Ireland
16.10.88: 22-**5-5**-10-24

Netherlands
29.10.88: 43-27-14-10-9-**3-3-3**-4-5-13-22-40-46-64-81

Sweden
30.11.88: 18-**12**-13-15-17 (bi-weekly)

Switzerland
6.11.88: 14-12-6-**4**-5-9-8-11-14-11-16-15-22-29

As she had with *You Came*, Kim co-wrote *Never Trust A Stranger* with her brother Ricky, and she recorded the song for her *CLOSE* album.

Never Trust A Stranger was released as the third single from the album and, like *You Came* before it, it was a sizeable hit in most countries. The single charted at no.2 in Denmark, no.3 in Finland and the Netherlands, no.4 in Switzerland, no.5 in Ireland, no.6 in Belgium, no.7 in Austria and the UK, no.11 in Germany, no.12 in Sweden and no.20 in France.

21 ~ Four Letter Word

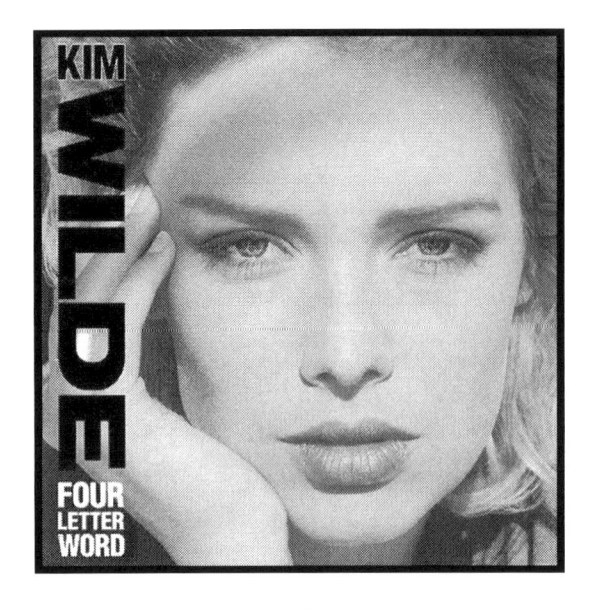

UK: MCA Records KIM 10 (1988).
  B-side: *She Hasn't Got Time For You '88*.

3.12.88: 51-34-28-19-14-9-**6**-12-18-30-45-73

Austria
15.04.89: **23-23** (bi-weekly)

Belgium
28.01.89: 27-22-17-14-12-12-**9**-14-29-34

Denmark
27.01.89: 15-10-11-**9**-12

Germany
13.02.89: 45-39-32-**27**-30-38-44-64-66-74

Ireland
11.12.88: 26-27-x-x-12-**5**-14-24-30

Netherlands
28.01.89: 69-34-15-10-**9-9**-17-27-46-64-83

Switzerland
26.02.89: **18**-x-**18**-21-22

Four Letter Word was written by Ricky & Marty Wilde, and was recorded by Kim for her *CLOSE* album.

Four Letter Word, unusually for Kim a straight ballad, was released as the fourth single from *CLOSE*, and it maintained Kim's run of success in many countries. The single achieved no.5 in Ireland, no.6 in the UK, no.9 in Belgium, Denmark and the Netherlands, no.18 in Switzerland, no.23 in Austria and no.27 in Germany.

22 ~ Love In The Natural Way

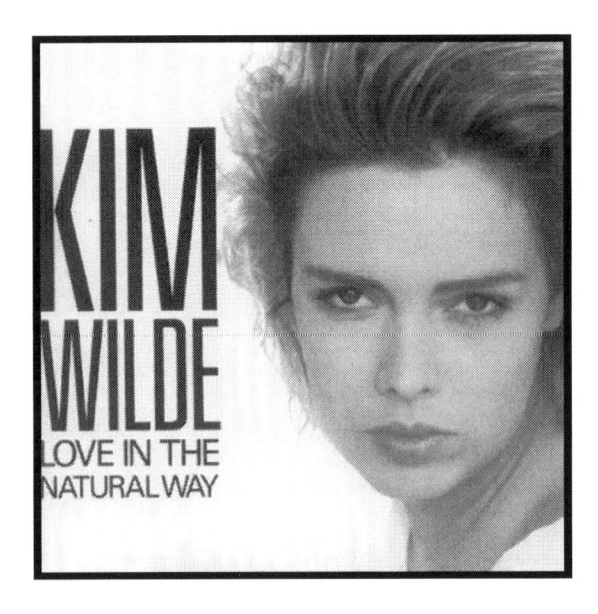

UK: MCA Records KIM 11 (1989).
B-side: *You'll Be The One Who'll Lose*.

4.03.89: 52-41-36-**32**-41-52

Ireland
12.03.89: **26**-28

Netherlands
15.04.89: 84-75-**63-63**-80

Kim co-wrote *Love In The Natural Way* with her brother Ricky and father Marty, and she recorded the song for her *CLOSE* album.
 Love In The Natural Way was released as the fifth and final single from the album. Not surprisingly, given how many people had already bought the album, *Love In The Natural Way* couldn't match the success of Kim's four previous singles from *CLOSE*, but it did achieve no.26 in Ireland, no.32 in the UK and no.63 in the Netherlands.
 Kim ended the decade as the most successful British female artist of the 1980s in the UK.

23 ~ It's Here

UK: MCA Records KIM 12 (1990).
 B-side: *Virtual World*.

14.04.90: 52-49-**42**-46

Australia
25.06.90: peaked at no.**92**, charted for 2 weeks

Belgium
9.06.90: **32**

Denmark
20.04.90: 7-**6-6**-8-7-7

Finland
04.90: peaked at no.**5**, charted for 4 weeks

Germany
30.04.90: 54-59-25-23-**21**-22-23-30-37-45-54-53-61-64-59-75-76-92-66

Netherlands
14.04.90: 87-69-60-74-61-55-49-43-**39**-57-90

Norway
5.05.90: 8-8-**6**-9

Sweden
9.05.90: 20-14-**13** (bi-weekly)

Switzerland
29.04.90: 18-17-21-18-**14**-15-15-16-18-29

Kim co-wrote *It's Here* with her brother Ricky, and she recorded the song for her 1990 album, *LOVE MOVES*.

It's Here was released as the lead single from the album, and was a moderate success, proving most popular in Scandinavia where it achieved no.5 in Finland, no.6 in Denmark and Norway and no.13 in Sweden. Elsewhere, the single was less successful, charting at no.14 in Switzerland, no.21 in Germany, no.32 in Belgium, no.39 in the Netherlands and no.42 in the UK.

In the UK only, Kim followed *It's Here* with another track from *LOVE MOVES*, *Time* – it struggled to no.71, thus becoming Kim's first single that failed to achieve Top 40 status anywhere.

24 ~ Can't Get Enough (Of Your Love)

UK: Not Released.

Europe: MCA Records 2292-57246-7 (1990).
  B-side: *Someday*.

France
7.07.90: 43-37-39-44-29-29-26-24-25-22-**21-21**-30-33-36-44

Germany
20.08.90: 93-x-**58**-88-87-x-93

Kim co-wrote *Can't Get Enough (Of You Love)* with Ricky, and she recorded the song for her *LOVE MOVES* album.

Can't Get Enough (Of Your Love) was released as the follow-up to *It's Here* in Australia and continental Europe, excluding France, where it was the first single lifted from the album. France was also the only country where the single achieved Top 40 status, peaking at no.21.

Can't Get Enough (Of Your Love) was also a minor no.58 hit in Germany, but it failed to chart anywhere else.

25 ~ Love Is Holy

UK: MCA Records KIM 15 (1992).
  B-side: *Birthday Song*.

2.05.92: 26-**16**-17-30-37-62

Australia
15.06.92: peaked at no.**39**, charted for 13 weeks

Austria
7.06.92: **28**

Belgium
13.06.92: 40-**23**-40-24-25-40-50

France
18.07.92: 45-48-47-42-**40**-48

Germany
25.05.92: 55-54-46-**42**-48-44-46-59-67-73-69-69-82

Ireland
25.05.92: **26**

Netherlands
2.05.92: 74-52-42-26-24-22-**21**-**21**-29-39-58-94

Sweden
10.06.92: **39**

Switzerland
25.04.92: 24-27-**13**-**13**-21-18-26-27-32-31-35-38

Love Is Holy was written by Ellen Shipley and Rick Nowels, and was recorded by Kim for her 1992 album, *LOVE IS*.

Following the poor sales of the singles from her previous album, *LOVE MOVES*, as the lead single from her new album, *Love Is Holy* gave Kim her biggest hit of the 1990s so far. The single charted at no.13 in Switzerland, no.16 in the UK, no.21 in the Netherlands, no.23 in Belgium, no.26 in Ireland, no.28 in Austria, no.39 in Australia and Sweden, no.40 in France and no.42 in Germany.

26 ~ Heart Over Mind

UK: MCA Records KIM 16 (1992).
  B-side: *I've Found A Reason*.

27.06.92: 48-**34**-49

Heart Over Mind was written by David Munday, John Hall, Nick Whitecross and Sandy Stewart, and it was the last track Kim recorded for her *LOVE IS* album.

Heart Over Mind was exclusively released as a single in the UK, where it spent a solitary week inside the Top 40 at no.34, during a brief three week chart run.

27 ~ If I Can't Have You

UK: MCA Records KIM 18 (1993).
 B-side: *Never Felt So Alive*.

10.07.93: 16-**12**-**12**-16-22-41-61-70

Australia
30.08.93: peaked at no.**2**, charted for 24 weeks

Austria
12.09.93: **29**

Belgium
14.08.93: 34-22-22-10-10-8-7-**6**-7-8-12-32

Germany
16.08.93: **51**-**51**-**51**-55-55-52-59-53-61-56-56-70-80-80

Ireland
18.07.93: 16-**9**-19-23-30

Netherlands
21.08.93: 37-26-**18**-21-27-43

Sweden
11.08.93: 39-x-x-x-30-30-**24**-x-x-x-33

Kim Wilde. If I Can't Have You

Words & Music by Barry Gibb, Maurice Gibb & Robin Gibb.
Recorded by Kim Wilde on MCA Records. Published by Gibb Brothers Music.
£1.95

Switzerland
1.08.93: 28-29-**18**-21-24-23-21-27-32-39-40-40

If I Can't Have You was composed by Barry, Maurice & Robin Gibb, and was recorded by Yvonne Elliman for the soundtrack of the 1977 film, *Saturday Night Fever*. The Bee Gees' own version of the song was issued as the B-side of their 1977 single, *Stayin' Alive*.

Yvonne Elliman took *If I Can't Have You* to no.1 in Canada and the United States, no.4 in the UK, no.5 in France, no.6 in New Zealand and no.9 in Australia and Ireland.

Having decided it was time to release her first approved 'greatest hits' album, which was titled *THE SINGLES COLLECTION 1981-1993*, Kim felt it was vital to support the compilation with a new hit single.

'We wanted to set it up properly,' she said. 'I didn't want to throw away thirteen years of success with a no.75 record. So we worked really hard writing material but, quite frankly, we weren't coming up with the kind of material that we felt would get us back into the charts – and so we decided to do a cover ... take a slightly less dangerous route.'

The cover they eventually settled on was *If I Can't Have You*.

'We went through the *Guinness Book of Hit Singles* and our record collection,' said Kim. 'It was Ricky's wife who suggested *If I Can't Have You*. I'd always thought it was one of the classier songs on the *Saturday Night Fever* soundtrack – it transcended it in many ways – so we tried it and it worked.'

If I Can't Have You was only the second cover Kim released as a single, after the hugely successful *You Keep Me Hangin' On*. The ploy worked, and Kim's version of the song achieved no.2 in Australia, no.6 in Belgium, no.9 in Ireland, no.12 in the UK, no.18 in the Netherlands and Switzerland, no.24 in Sweden, no.29 in Austria and no.51 in Germany.

28 ~ Loved

UK: EMI 7243 5 50235 2 0 (2001).
 B-side: *Kids In America (D-Bop's Bright Lights Mix*.

Loved wasn't a hit in the UK.

Belgium
24.11.01: 32-21-12-**7**-**7**-9-11-14-15-19-29-42

Finland
26.01.02: **19**

Sweden
25.01.02: 58-**45**-55-47-56

Switzerland
2.12.01: 85-**68**-83-x-x-69

Written by Ricki Wilde and Terry Ronald, *Loved* was recorded by Kim for her 2001 compilation album, *THE VERY BEST OF KIM WILDE*.
 Released as a s ingle to promote the compilation, *Loved* achieved no.7 in Belgium, no.19 in Finland, no.45 in Sweden and no.68 in in Switzerland, but it failed to chart in many countries, including the UK.

29 ~ Anyplace, Anywhere, Anytime

Europe: WSM 5050466-8220-2-5 (2003).
  Tracks: *Anyplace, Anywhere, Anytime (Radio Version)/(New Version)*.

Austria
1.06.03: 9-4-2-**1**-2-4-4-5-7-9-15-19-25-30-41-54-67-66-70

Belgium
18.10.03: 34-11-7-6-3-**2**-4-4-5-7-9-10-11-10-14-20-21-33-42

Denmark
22.08.03: **19**

Germany
2.06.03: 5-7-**3-3**-5-6-11-14-18-21-31-37-42-54-58

Netherlands
16.08.03: 52-47-36-19-15-8-5-2-2-**1-1-1-1**-2-2-3-5-8-12-19-20-21-31-45-51-65-57-69-76

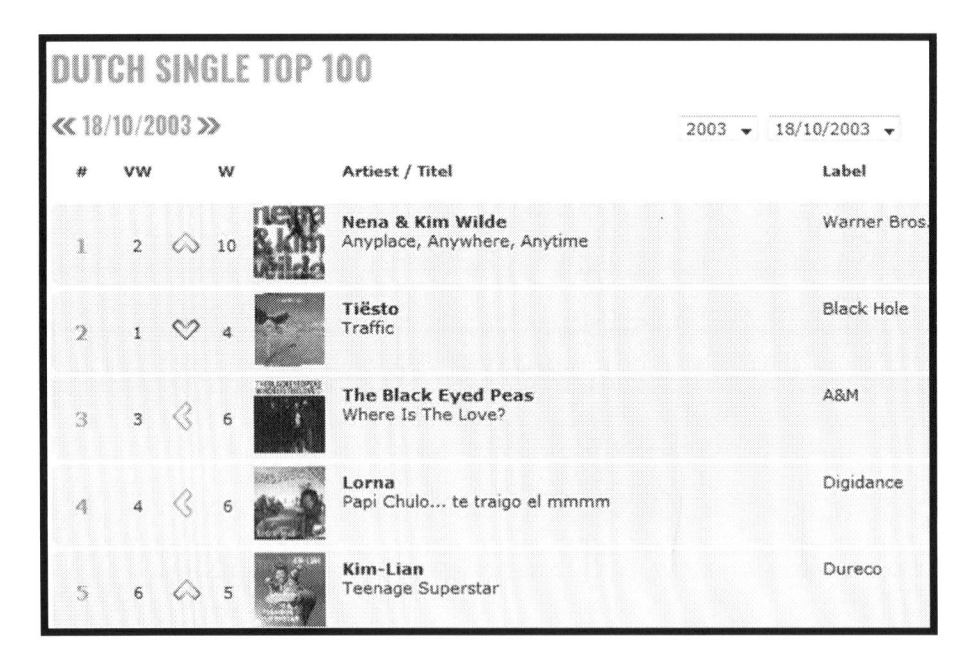

#	VW	W		Artiest / Titel	Label
1	2	⌂ 10		Nena & Kim Wilde — Anyplace, Anywhere, Anytime	Warner Bros.
2	1	♡ 4		Tiësto — Traffic	Black Hole
3	3	‹ 6		The Black Eyed Peas — Where Is The Love?	A&M
4	4	‹ 6		Lorna — Papi Chulo... te traigo el mmmm	Digidance
5	6	⌂ 5		Kim-Lian — Teenage Superstar	Dureco

DUTCH SINGLE TOP 100 « 18/10/2003 » — 2003, 18/10/2003

Switzerland
8.06.03: 51-17-18-17-15-13-11-**9**-11-11-15-18-22-33-43-63-67-76-81-100-x-93

Irgendwie, Irgendwo, Irgendwann was composed by Carlo Karges and Uwe Fahrenkrog-Petersen, and was recorded by the German band Nena for their 1984 album, *FEUER UND FLAMME* (Fire And Flame'). The original version of the song charted at no.2 in Switzerland, no.3 in Germany, no.7 in Austria and no.13 in the Netherlands.

Nena, best known for the 1983/84 hit *99 Luftballons* (aka *99 Red Balloons*), recorded an English version of the song, with lyrics by Lisa Dalbello, for the 1985 album, *IT'S ALL IN THE GAME* – this version of the song wasn't released as a single.

In 2002, the band's lead singer Nena released an album titled *NENA FEAT. NENA*, which featured a duet version of *Anyplace, Anywhere, Anytime*, with Nena singing in German and Kim singing in English.

The duet version of *Anyplace, Anywhere, Anytime* was issued as a single in continental Europe, but not the UK, and Kim and Nena first performed the song live in Frankfurt, Germany, in October 2002, at a concert that marked the twentieth anniversary of Nena's first hit. To promote the single, Kim and Nena filmed a music video in London, and appeared together on several TV shows in Europe.

Anyplace, Anywhere, Anytime hit no.1 in Austria and the Netherlands, and achieved no.2 in Belgium, no.3 in Germany, no.9 in Switzerland and no.19 in Denmark.

To celebrate Nena's 50th birthday, Kim joined her in 2010 to perform *Anyplace, Anywhere, Anytime* on a German TV show. Four years later, during a joint concert in Saasveld, the Netherlands, on 13th December 2014, Kim and Nena performed the song live on stage.

30 ~ Run To You

UK: Not Released.

Scandinavia: Universal Music (digital release, 2009)

Sweden
11.09.09: **24**-26-43-59

Kim recorded *Run To You* with the Swedish funk rock band Fibes, Oh Fibes! for their 2009 album, *1987*.

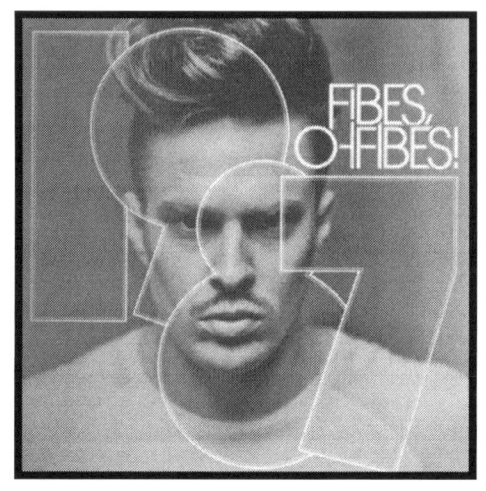

Released as a digital single in Scandinavia only, *Run To You* made its chart debut at no.24 in Sweden, but it climbed no higher.

31 ~ Lights Down Low

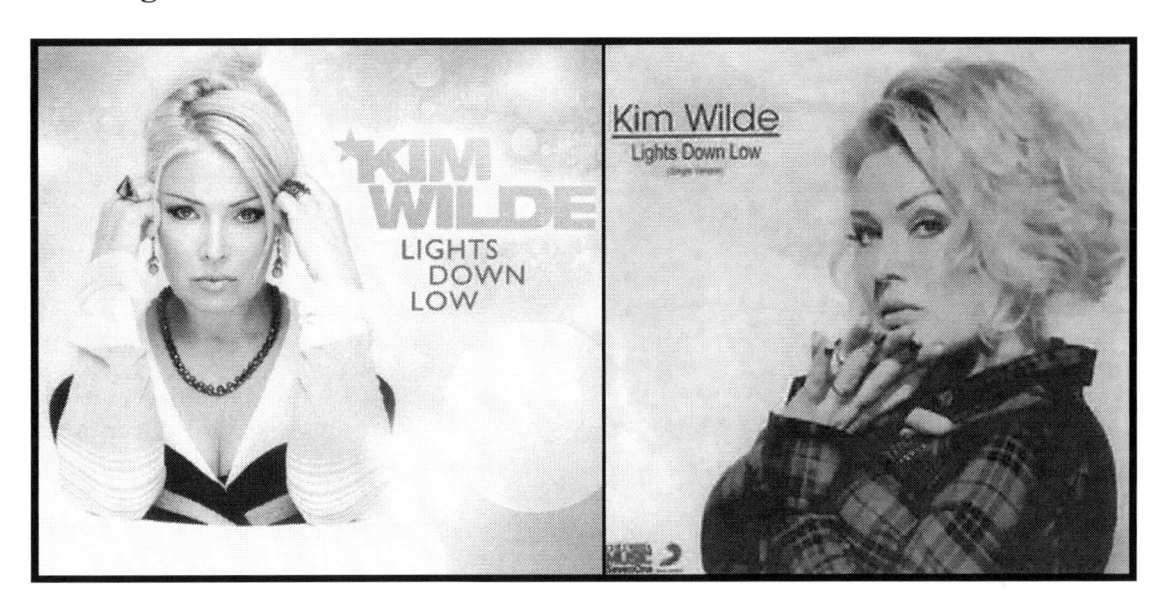

UK: Columbia SevenOne Music (digital release, 2010).

Lights Down Low wasn't a hit in the UK.

Germany: Columbia SevenOne Music 88697758212 (2010).
  B-side: *Snakes & Ladders*.

27.08.10: **34**-52-38-41-46-52-65-74-81

Switzerland
12.09.10: **62**

Lights Down Low was written by Anthony Galatis and Mark Frisch, and was recorded by Kim for her 2010 album, *COME OUT AND PLAY*.
  Lights Down Low was released as the album's lead single, however, it was only issued as a CD single in France and Germany, and was released digitally elsewhere. The single achieved Top 40 status in one country, Germany, where it made its chart debut at no.34. *Lights Down Low* was a minor no.62 hit in Switzerland, but it failed to chart in most countries, including the UK.

THE ALMOST TOP 40 SINGLES

Three of Kim's singles have achieved Top 50 status in one or more countries, but failed to enter the Top 40 in any.

Who Do You Think You Are?

Kim co-wrote *Who Do You Think You Are?* with her brother Ricky, and recorded the song for her 1992 album, *LOVE IS*. A remixed version of the song was released as the second international single from the album, after *Love Is Holy* (*Heart Over Mind* was exclusively issued as the second single in the UK). *Who Do You Think You Are?* achieved no.49 in the UK, no.58 in Germany and no.66 in the Netherlands, but it failed to enter the Top 40 anywhere.

Breakin' Away

Breakin' Away was composed by Tracy Ackerman, Mike Percy and Tim Lever, and Kim recorded the song for her 1995 album, *NOW & FOREVER*. *Breakin' Away* was released as the lead single from the album, but only managed to chart at no.43 in the UK and no.79 in Germany, and it failed to achieve Top 40 status anywhere.

This I Swear

This I Swear was written by Tony Swain and Pam Sheyne, and was recorded by Kim for her 1995 album, *NOW & FOREVER*. Like *Breakin' Away*, which preceded it as a single, *This I Swear* missed the Top 40 in the only two countries where it charted, stalling at no.46 in the UK and no.91 in Germany.

Note: to date, none of Kim's albums have achieved Top 50 status in one or more countries, but failed to enter the Top 40 in any.

KIM'S TOP 25 SINGLES

In this Top 25, each of Kim's Top 40 singles has been scored according to the following points system.

Points are given according to the peak position reached on the albums chart in each of the countries featured in this book:

No.1:	100 points for the first week at no.1, plus 10 points for each additional week at no.1.
No.2:	90 points for the first week at no.2, plus 5 points for each additional week at no.2.
No.3:	85 points.
No.4-6:	80 points.
No.7-10:	75 points.
No.11-15:	70 points.
No.16-20:	65 points.
No.21-30:	60 points.
No.31-40:	50 points.
No.41-50:	40 points.
No.51-60:	30 points.
No.61-70:	20 points.
No.71-80:	10 points.
No.81-100:	5 points.

Total weeks charted in each country are added, to give the final points score.

Reissues, re-entries and re-recordings of a single are counted together.

Rank/Single/Points

1 *Cambodia* – 1780 points

2 *Kids In America* – 1746 points

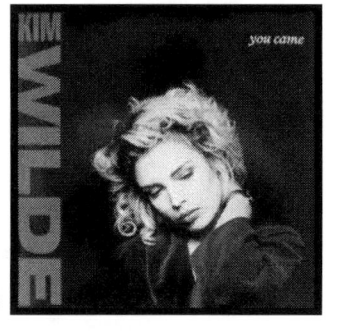

3 *You Came* – 1442 points

4 *You Keep Me Hangin' On* – 1215 points

VIDEO 7

KIM WILDE

NEIGE
UN FESTIVAL VIDEO A ISOLA 2000

SCOOP
LA MORT D'UN TRUAND FILMEE EN DIRECT !

CLIPS
DES IMAGES FOLLES PAR DES GENS DINGUES

STAR
UN SEXE NOMME KIM WILDE

VEGAS
PUCES ROBOTS, LASERS ET COMPAGNIE

Rank/Single/Points

5 *Chequered Love* – 1195 points

6. *View From A Bridge* – 1183 points
7. *Never Trust A Stranger* – 990 points
8. *Love Blonde* – 836 points
9. *If I Can't Have You* – 682 points
10. *Anyplace, Anywhere, Anytime* – 649 points

11. *It's Here* – 647 points
12. *Love Is Holy* – 637 points
13. *Four Letter Word* – 633 points
14. *Hey Mister Heartache* – 624 points
15. *Child Come Away* – 553 points

16. *The Second Time* – 496 points
17. *Dancing In The Dark* – 427 points
18. *Rockin' Around The Christmas Tree* – 335 points
19. *The Touch* – 229 points
20. *Loved* – 222 points

21. *Schoolgirl* – 195 points
21. *Another Step (Closer To You)* – 195 points
23. *Say You Really Want Me* – 180 points
24. *Water On Glass* – 157 points
25. *Love In The Natural Way* – 143 points

A narrow, and perhaps surprising, victory for *Cambodia*, which emerges as Kim's most successful single ahead of her debut, *Kids In America*.

You Came, even with the 2006 version included, is more than 300 points adrift in third place, with *You Keep Me Hangin' On* and *Chequered Love* rounding off the Top 5.

Kim's most recent single to make the Top 25 is her 2003 collaboration with Nena, *Anyplace, Anywhere, Anytime*, which is at no.10.

SINGLES TRIVIA

To date, Kim has achieved 31 Top 40 singles in one or more of the countries featured in this book.

There follows a country-by-country look at Kim's most successful hits, starting with her homeland.

Note: in the past, there was often one or more weeks over Christmas and New Year when no new chart was published in some countries. In such cases, the previous week's chart has been used to complete chart runs. Similarly, where a bi-weekly or monthly chart was in place, for chart runs these are counted as two and four weeks, respectively.

KIM WILDE IN THE UK

Kim has achieved 31 hit singles in the UK, which spent 196 weeks on the chart.

Her most successful singles are *Kids In America* and *You Keep Me Hangin' On*, which both spent two weeks at no.2.

Singles with the most weeks

14 weeks	*You Keep Me Hangin' On*
13 weeks	*Kids In America*
12 weeks	*Cambodia*
12 weeks	*Four Letter Word*
11 weeks	*Another Step Closer To You*
11 weeks	*You Came*
9 weeks	*Chequered Love*
9 weeks	*Never Trust A Stranger*
8 weeks	*Water On Glass / Boys*
8 weeks	*Love Blonde*
8 weeks	*Rage To Love*
8 weeks	*Rockin' Around The Christmas Tree*
8 weeks	*If I Can't Have You*

The Brit Certified/BPI (British Phonographic Industry) Awards

The BPI began certifying Silver, Gold & Platinum singles in 1973. From 1973 to 1988: Silver = 250,000, Gold = 500,000 & Platinum = 1 million. From 1989 onwards: Silver = 200,000, Gold = 400,000 & Platinum = 600,000. Awards are based on shipments, not sales; however, in July 2013 the BPI automated awards, based on actual sales since February 1994.

Gold	*Kids In America* (April 1981)	= 500,000
Silver	*Chequered Love* (May 1981)	= 250,000
Silver	*You Keep Me Hangin' On* (November 1986)	= 250,000
Silver	*Rockin' Around The Christmas Tree* (January 1988)	= 250,000
Silver	*You Came* (October 1988)	= 250,000

KIM WILDE IN AUSTRALIA

Kim has achieved 15 hit singles in Australia, which spent 213 weeks on the chart.

No.1 Singles

1987   *You Keep Me Hangin' On*

You Keep Me Hangin' On topped the chart for two weeks.

Singles with the most weeks

28 weeks	*You Keep Me Hangin' On*
25 weeks	*Kids In America*
24 weeks	*Cambodia*
24 weeks	*If I Can't Have You*
21 weeks	*Chequered Love*
21 weeks	*You Came*
20 weeks	*View From A Bridge*
14 weeks	*Love Blonde*
13 weeks	*Love Is Holy*

KIM WILDE IN AUSTRIA

Kim has achieved 11 hit singles in Austria, which spent 117 weeks on the chart.

No.1 Singles

2003   *Anyplace, Anywhere, Anytime*

Anyplace, Anywhere, Anytime topped the chart for one week.

Singles with the most weeks

30 weeks	*You Came*
19 weeks	*Anyplace, Anywhere, Anytime*
14 weeks	*Cambodia*
12 weeks	*View From A Bridge*
12 weeks	*Never Trust A Stranger*
10 weeks	*You Keep Me Hangin' On*
8 weeks	*Kids in America*

KIM WILDE IN BELGIUM (Flanders)

Kim has achieved 19 hit singles in Belgium (Flanders), which spent 181 weeks on the chart.

Her most successful singles are *Chequered Love*, *Cambodia* and *Anyplace, Anywhere, Anytime*, which all peaked at no.2.

Singles with the most weeks

19 weeks	*Anyplace, Anywhere, Anytime*
18 weeks	*Cambodia*
16 weeks	*You Came*
14 weeks	*Never Trust A Stranger*
13 weeks	*Kids In America*
12 weeks	*Chequered Love*
12 weeks	*If I Can't Have You*
12 weeks	*Loved*
10 weeks	*View From A Bridge*
10 weeks	*Four Letter Word*

KIM WILDE IN DENMARK

Kim has achieved 17 hit singles in Denmark, which spent 181 weeks on the chart.

No.1 Singles

1988	*You Came*

You Came topped the chart for four weeks.

Singles with the most weeks

23 weeks	*Cambodia*
19 weeks	*Chequered Love*
18 weeks	*Kids In America*
15 weeks	*View From A Bridge*
15 weeks	*You Came*
13 weeks	*Never Trust A Stranger*
12 weeks	*Dancing In The Dark*
12 weeks	*Rockin' Around The Christmas Tree*
9 weeks	*The Second Time*

KIM WILDE IN FINLAND

Kim has achieved 10 hit singles in Finland, which spent 96 weeks on the chart

No.1 Singles

1981   *Kids In America*

Kids In America topped the chart for two weeks

Singles with the most weeks

26 weeks	*Kids In America*
12 weeks	*Cambodia*
12 weeks	*View From A Bridge*
12 weeks	*Love Blonde*
12 weeks	*You Came*
8 weeks	*Dancing In The Dark*
8 weeks	*Never Trust A Stranger*

KIM WILDE IN FRANCE

Kim has achieved 11 hits singles in France, which spent 285 weeks on the chart

No.1 Singles

1982   *Cambodia*

Cambodia topped the chart for 14 weeks

Singles with the most weeks

44 weeks	*Kids In America*
34 weeks	*Cambodia*
23 weeks	*Love Blonde*
23 weeks	*You Came*
22 weeks	*View From A Bridge*
17 weeks	*You Keep Me Hangin' On*
16 weeks	*Can't Get Enough (Of Your Love)*
14 weeks	*Never Trust A Stranger*
13 weeks	*Child Come Away*

KIM WILDE IN GERMANY

Kim has achieved 29 hit singles in Germany, which spent 363 weeks on the chart.

Her most successful singles are *Chequered Love* and *Cambodia*, which both peaked at no.2.

Singles with the most weeks

32 weeks	*Kids In America*
26 weeks	*Cambodia*
26 weeks	*You Came*
24 weeks	*Chequered Love*
19 weeks	*View From A Bridge*
19 weeks	*It's Here*
15 weeks	*Love Blonde*
15 weeks	*The Second Time*
15 weeks	*Never Trust A Stranger*
15 weeks	*Anyplace, Anywhere, Anytime*

KIM WILDE IN IRELAND

Kim has achieved 17 hit singles in Ireland, which spent 88 weeks on the chart.

Her most successful singles are *Kids In America* and *You Keep Me Hangin' On*, which both peaked at no.2.

Singles with the most weeks

9 weeks	*Kids In America*
8 weeks	*Cambodia*
8 weeks	*Another Step (Closer To You)*
8 weeks	*Rockin' Around The Christmas Tree*
8 weeks	*You Came*
7 weeks	*Chequered Love*
7 weeks	*You Keep Me Hangin' On*
7 weeks	*Four Letter Word*

KIM WILDE IN ITALY

Kim has achieved two hit singles in Italy, which spent 40 weeks on the chart.

Her most successful single is *You Came, which peaked at no.3.*

Singles with the most weeks

24 weeks	*You Came*
16 weeks	*Hey Mister Heartache*

KIM WILDE IN JAPAN

Kim has achieved two hit singles in Japan, which spent 17 weeks on the chart.

Her most successful single is *Bitter Is Better*, which peaked at no.58.

Singles with the most weeks

12 weeks   *Bitter Is Better*
 5 weeks   *You Keep Me Hangin' On*

KIM WILDE IN THE NETHERLANDS

Kim has achieved 21 hit singles in the Netherlands, which spent 214 weeks on the chart.

No.1 Singles

2003   *Anyplace, Anywhere, Anytime*

Anyplace, Anywhere, Anytime topped the chart for four weeks.

Singles with the most weeks

29 weeks   *Anyplace, Anywhere, Anytime*
26 weeks   *You Came*
17 weeks   *Never Trust A Stranger*
16 weeks   *Cambodia*
14 weeks   *Kids In America*
12 weeks   *Love Is Holy*
11 weeks   *You Keep Me Hangin' On*
11 weeks   *Four Letter Word*
11 weeks   *It's Here*
10 weeks   *Hey Mister Heartache*

KIM WILDE IN NEW ZEALAND

Kim has achieved three hit singles in New Zealand, which spent 38 weeks on the chart.

Her most successful single is *Kids In America*, which peaked at no.5.

Singles with the most weeks

20 weeks   *You Keep Me Hangin' On*
14 weeks   *Kids In America*
 4 weeks   *Cambodia*

KIM WILDE IN NORWAY

Kim has achieved seven hit singles in Norway, which spent 52 weeks on the chart.

No.1 Singles

1987   *You Keep Me Hangin' On*

You Keep Me Hangin' On topped the chart for three weeks.

Singles with the most weeks

14 weeks   *Cambodia*
11 weeks   *Hey Mister Heartache*
10 weeks   *You Keep Me Hangin' On*
10 weeks   *You Came*

KIM WILDE IN SOUTH AFRICA

Kim achieved three hit singles in South Africa, which spent 42 weeks on the chart.

No.1 Singles

1981   *Kids In America*
1981   *Chequered Love*

Both singles topped the chart for one week.

Singles with the most weeks

16 weeks   *Cambodia*
15 weeks   *Kids In America*
11 weeks   *Chequered Love*

KIM WILDE IN SWEDEN

Kim has achieved 13 hit singles in Sweden, which spent 123 weeks on the chart.

No.1 Singles

1982   *Cambodia*

Cambodia topped the chart for four weeks.

Singles with the most weeks

22 weeks	*Cambodia*
18 weeks	*Kids In America*
16 weeks	*You Came*
12 weeks	*View From A Bridge*
10 weeks	*Never Trust A Stranger*
8 weeks	*Chequered Love*
8 weeks	*Child Come Away*
8 weeks	*Love Blonde*

KIM WILDE IN SWITZERLAND

Kim has achieved 20 hit singles in Sweden, which spent 203 weeks on the chart.

No.1 Singles

1982   *Cambodia*

Cambodia topped the chart for two weeks.

Singles with the most weeks

27 weeks	*You Came*
21 weeks	*Anyplace, Anywhere, Anytime*
14 weeks	*Never Trust A Stranger*
12 weeks	*Cambodia*
12 weeks	*The Second Time*
12 weeks	*Hey Mister Heartache*
12 weeks	*Love Is Holy*
12 weeks	*If I Can't Have You*
11 weeks	*Kids In America*
11 weeks	*View From A Bridge*

KIM WILDE IN THE USA

Kim has achieved five hit singles in the United States, which spent 64 weeks on the chart.

No.1 Singles

1987   *You Keep Me Hangin' On*

You Keep Me Hangin' On topped the chart for one week.

Singles with the most Hot 100 weeks

21 weeks   *You Keep Me Hangin' On*
18 weeks   *Kids In America*
10 weeks   *You Came*
 8 weeks   *Say You Really Want Me*
 7 weeks   *Go For It*

RIAA (Recording Industry Association of America) Awards

The RIAA began certifying Gold singles in 1958 and Platinum singles in 1976. From 1958 to 1988: Gold = 1 million, Platinum = 2 million. From 1988 onwards: Gold = 500,000, Platinum = 1 million. Awards are based on shipments, not sales (unless the award is for digital sales).

None of Kim's singles have been certified in the United States.

KIM WILDE IN ZIMBABWE

Kim has achieved four hit singles in Zimbabwe, which spent 36 weeks on the chart.

No.1 Singles

1981   *Kids In America*

Kids In America topped the chart for one week.

Singles with the most weeks

17 weeks   *Kids In America*
 8 weeks   *Chequered Love*
 6 weeks   *View From A Bridge*
 5 weeks   *Cambodia*

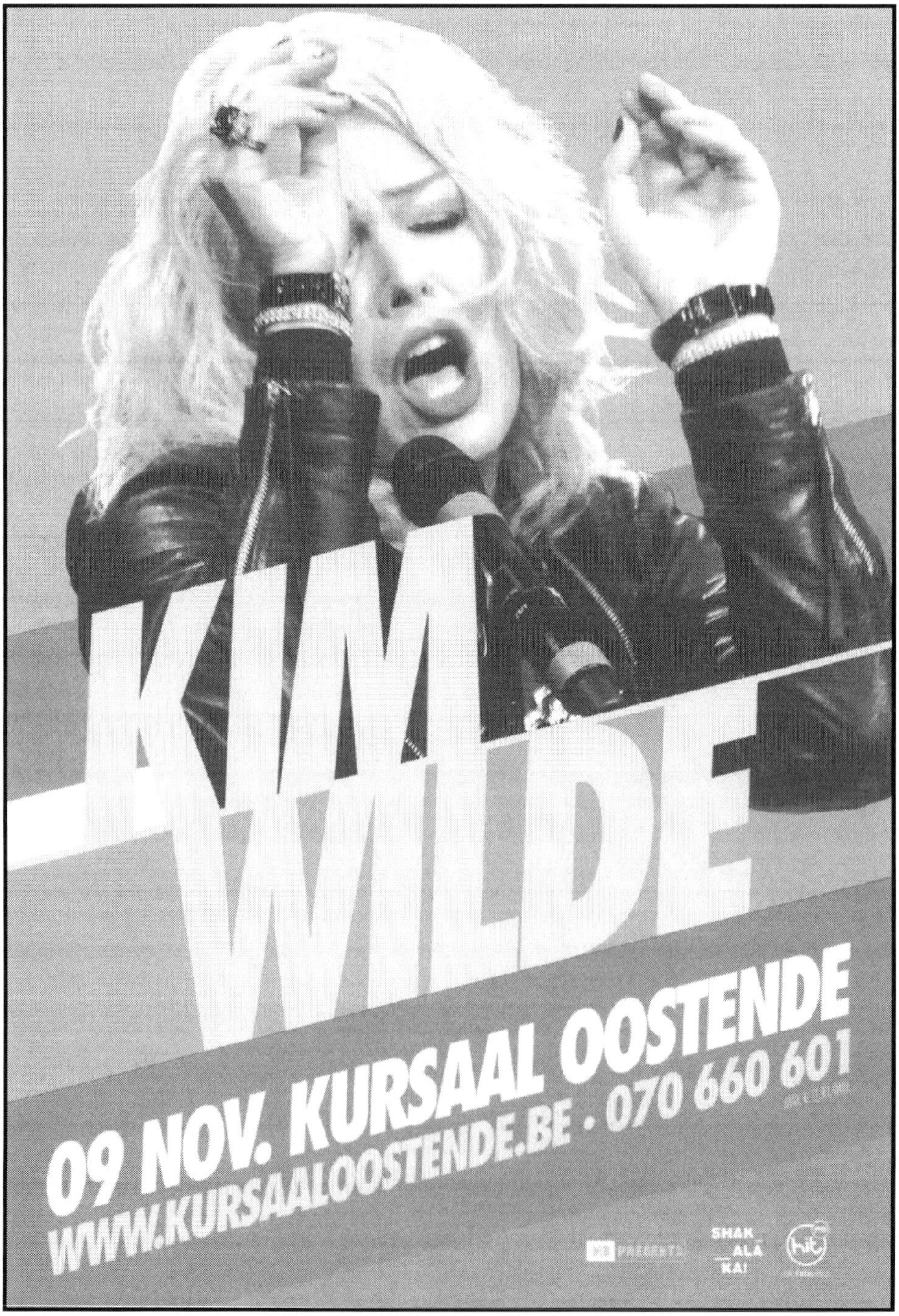
KIM
WILDE
09 NOV. KURSAAL OOSTENDE
WWW.KURSAALOOSTENDE.BE . 070 660 601
SHAK ALA KA!

All The Top 40 Albums

ZIG ZAG

No 122 February 82 60p $2.00

**STEVE SEVERIN
ORANGE JUICE
THE DAMNED
COLD FISH**

**CRASS
KIM WILDE**

EXCLUSIVE ECHO & THE BUNNYMEN VIDEO OFFER INSIDE!

1 ~ KIM WILDE

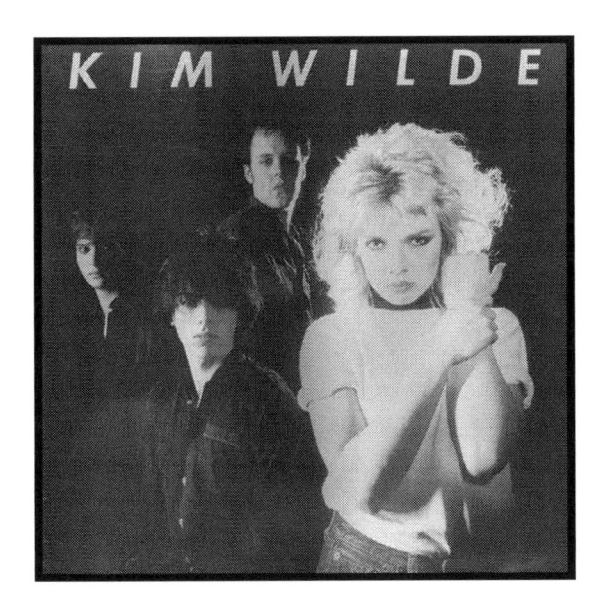

Water On Glass/Our Town/Everything We Know/Young Heroes/Kids In America/ Chequered Love/2-6-5-8-0/You'll Never Be So Wrong/Falling Out/Tuning In Tuning On

Produced by Ricky Wilde.

UK: RAK SRAK 544 (1981).

11.07.81: 10-**3**-5-4-12-8-11-9-12-19-34-46-94-93

Australia
17.08.81: peaked at no.**25**, charted for 15 weeks

Finland
07.81: peaked at no.**3**, charted for 20 weeks

Japan
21.11.81: peaked at no.**59**, charted for 4 weeks

Netherlands
18.07.81: 6-**5**-14-12-17-14-11-17-17-50-41-x-45
13.02.82: 46-45

New Zealand
30.08.81: **39**-50

KIM WILDE.

ONLY 3.99.

THE HMV AMERICAN MUSIC MART
JULY 4 THRU JULY 18

HUNDREDS OF ALBUMS BY U.S. ARTISTS ALL AT ONLY 2.99 EACH INCLUDING...

The Band	Blue Oyster Cult	Bob Seger
Beach Boys	Bob Dylan	Boston
Billy Joel	...and that's only the B's!	

the HMV shop

Germany
20.07.81: 16-2-2-**1-1-1-1-1**-2-2-2-5-7-8-11-17-26-26-27-56-44-58-50-x-52-x-60-48-x-62-63-42-x-59-x-58

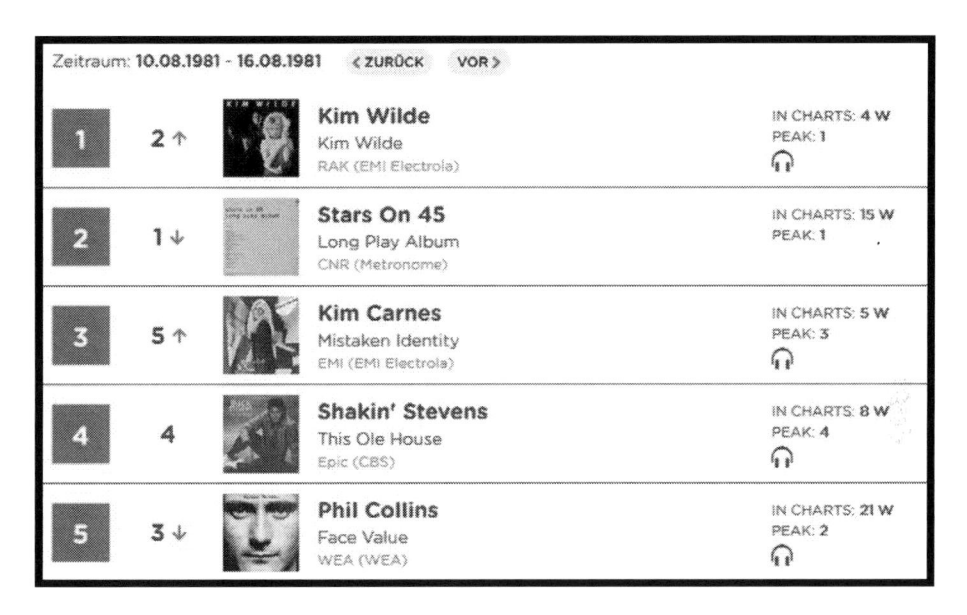

Sweden
3.07.81: 8-**1**-3-4-9-13-21-36-x-x-24-12-8-13-15-22-39 (bi-weekly)

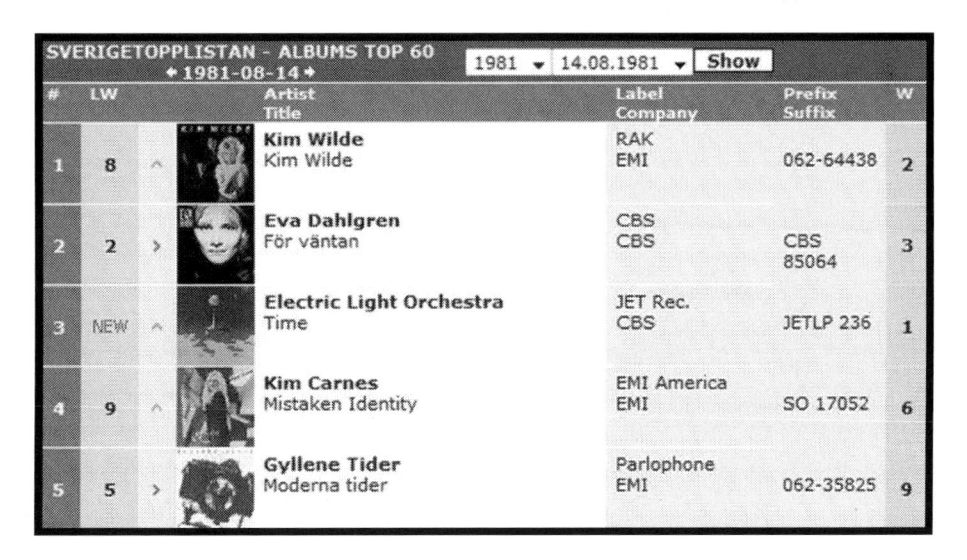

USA
17.07.82: 100-92-90-**86-86**

Kim recorded her self-titled debut album during 1980 and the first half of 1981 at London's RAK Studio and Lodge Studio. As well as Kim, the album's sleeve featured a photograph by Gered Mankowitz of the band Kim used for promotional purposes, namely her brother Ricky, Calvin Hayes and James Stevenson.

'It was supposed to look like that,' said Kim, 'like a British Blondie. I didn't want to be perceived as a solo singer, because that was passé at the time. and in my mind it wasn't just me, it was me and Ricky – we couldn't exactly have Dad on the cover!'

Nine of the ten songs on the album were written for Kim by her brother Ricky and dad Marty. The one exception, *Falling Out*, was a song Ricky composed on his own – he also produced the album.

The album featured three hit singles:

- *Kids In America*
- *Chequered Love*
- *Water On Glass*

KIM WILDE topped the chart in Germany for five straight weeks, and also hit no.1 in Sweden. The album achieved no.3 in Finland and the UK, no.5 in the Netherlands, no.25 in Australia and no.39 in New Zealand, but it was only a minor hit in Japan and the United States.

The album was remastered and reissued in Europe in 2009, with three bonus tracks: *Shane/Boys/Water On Glass (7" Version)*

Deluxe Edition

Kim's first three albums were each issued as a Deluxe Edition in 2020, comprising 2 x CDs and a DVD, plus as a coloured vinyl album.

CD1 Bonus Tracks: *Shane/Boys/Water On Glass (7" Version)/Tuning In Tuning On (7" Version)*

CD2: *Kids In America (Luke Mornay Remix)/Chequered Love (Matt Pop Extended Version)/Water On Glass (Eddie Said & Luke Nutley Extended Version)/Kids In America (Popfidelity Allstars Remix)/Chequered Love (Matt Pop Alternative Remix)/Water On Glass (Project: Project Kim)/Kids In America (Neutrophonic Remix)/(D-Bop's Bright Lights Mix)/Popfidelity Allstars Instrumental)/Chequered Love (Matt Pop Instrumental)/ Water On Glass (Eddie Said & Luke Nutley Instrumental)/Kids In America (Luke Mornay Instrumental)*

DVD: *Kids In America/Chequered Love/Kids In America (Top Of The Pops)/Chequered Love (Top Of The Pops)/Water On Glass (Top Of The Pops)/Kids In America (Top Of The Pops Christmas Party)/Chequered Love (Unedited Slower Version)*

At the same time, minus any bonus tracks, *KIM WILDE* was reissued on yellow vinyl.

2 ~ SELECT

Ego/Words Fell Down/Action City/View From A Bridge/Just A Feeling/Chaos At The Airport/Take Me Tonight/Can You Come Over/Wendy Sadd/Cambodia + Reprise

Produced by Ricky Wilde.

UK: RAK SRAK 548 (1982).

22.05.82: 25-**19**-22-31-33-53-59-82-65-63-92

Australia
19.07.82: peaked at no.**8**, charted for 12 weeks

Austria
15.07.82: **20** (bi-weekly)

Finland
05.82: peaked at no.**1** (3), charted for 26 weeks

Germany
7.06.82: 26-6-**4**-5-6-8-14-16-21-24-27-20-24-35-40-39-43-63-58

Japan
1.06.82: peaked at no.**27**, charted for 13 weeks

KIM WILDE
SELECT

NEW ALBUM NEW CASSETTE
SRAK548 TC/SRAK548

INCLUDES THE HIT SINGLES 'CAMBODIA' AND 'VIEW FROM A BRIDGE'

AVAILABLE FROM BOOTS RECORD DEPARTMENTS

SUBJECT TO STOCK AVAILABILITY

Netherlands
22.05.82: 11-**1**-2-4-11-19-21-29-38-46

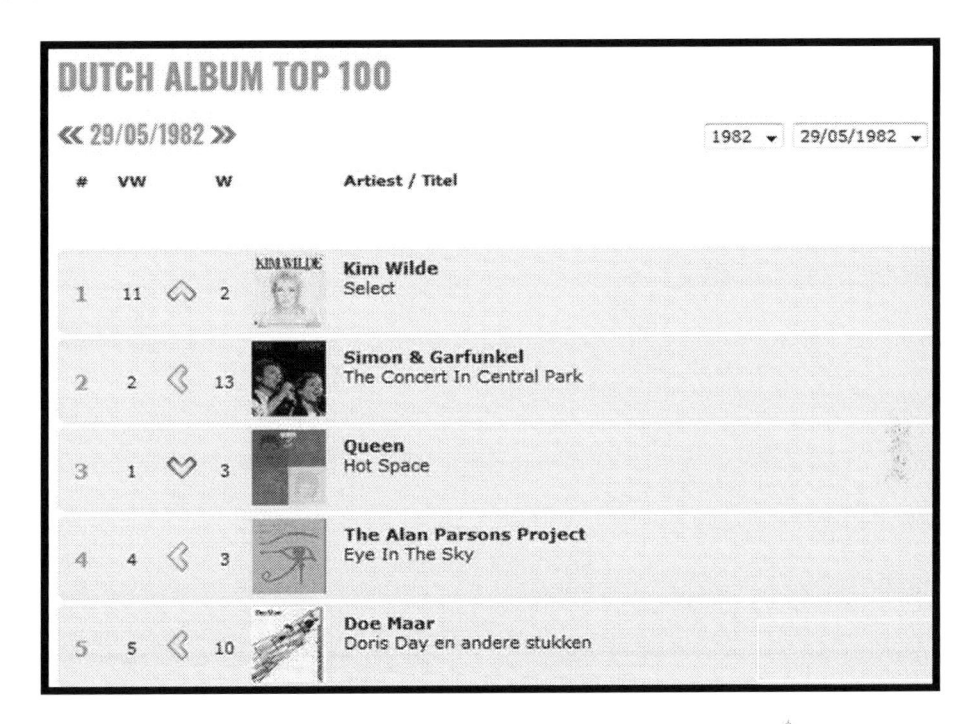

#	VW	W	Artiest / Titel
1	11	2	**Kim Wilde** — Select
2	2	13	**Simon & Garfunkel** — The Concert In Central Park
3	1	3	**Queen** — Hot Space
4	4	3	**The Alan Parsons Project** — Eye In The Sky
5	5	10	**Doe Maar** — Doris Day en andere stukken

DUTCH ALBUM TOP 100 — 29/05/1982

Norway
15.05.82: 26-26-20-17-19-26-30-30-**12**-17-22-27-36-37-36

Sweden
1.06.82: 5-**2**-3-3-8-11-16-32 (bi-weekly)
25.01.83: 48 (bi-weekly)

Following the success of her debut album, Kim said, 'It was a case of, "Let's do the next one", and we came up with *SELECT* … we weren't ready for the second album, which so often happens, not just for us but for a lot of acts.'

All ten tracks Kim recorded for the album were written by her brother Ricky and father Marty, with Ricky once again producing the album. The sleeve photograph was taken by Gered Mankowitz.

'I hated the sleeve for *SELECT*,' said Kim, 'because it was boring and a bit tacky. The actual shot was all right, but not the way it was presented. Now I've taken complete control of how I'm presented so what you see from now on, whether you like it or not, is me.'

Two singles were released from the album, and both were sizeable hits:

- *Cambodia*
- *View From A Bridge*

In most countries, *SELECT* couldn't quite match the success of *KIM WILDE*, but it did go to no.1 in both Finland and the Netherlands. Elsewhere, the album achieved no.2 in Sweden, no.4 in Germany, no.8 in Australia, no.12 in Norway, no.19 in the UK, no.20 in Austria and no.27 in Japan.

SELECT was remastered and reissued in Europe in 2009, with five bonus track:

Watching For Shapes/Cambodia (Single Version)/Child Come Away/Just Another Guy/Bitter Is Better

Deluxe Edition

The Deluxe Edition of *SELECT*, issued in Europe in 2020, comprised two CDs and a DVD:

CD1 Bonus Tracks: *Child Come Away/Bitter Is Better/He Will Be There/Watching For Shapes/Just Another Guy/Bitter Is Better (Instrumental)*

CD2: *Ego (Rough Mix)/Words Fell Down (Original Mix)/Action City (Instrumental Demo)/Just A Feeling (Rough Mix)/Chaos At The Airport (Rough Mix)/Take Me Tonight (Original Mix)/Cambodia (Matt Pop Extended Version)/View From A Bridge (Luke Mornay Remix)/Child Come Away (Matt Pop Remix)/Cambodia (Luke Mornay Urbantronik Mix)/View From A Bridge (RAW Remix)/Child Come Away (Matt Pop Instrumental)/Cambodia (Matt Pop Instrumental)/View From A Bridge (Luke Mornay Instrumental)/Cambodia (Luke Mornay Urbantronik Instrumental)*

DVD: *Cambodia/View From A Bridge/Child Come Away/Cambodia (Top Of The Pops)/View From A Bridge (Top Of The Pops)/(Nationwide Special: The British Rock & Pop Awards)*

At the same time, the original *SELECT* album was reissued on white vinyl.

THE FACE
NUMBER 23
THROBBING GRISTLE/PSYCHIC TELEVISION
SOAP · GERRY COONEY · PRACTICAL STYLING
PHOTO BY DAVIES/STARR

Nr. 37 3. September 1981 – DM 1,50 bei Hauslieferung zuzügl. Zustellgebühr · öS 13,– · hfr 4,50 · Lire 1000,– · Ptas 80,– · sfr 1,80 · Printed in Germany
C 1917 C
BRAVO
MIT FOTO-LOVE-STORY
Neuer Starschnitt:
ADAM ANT
in Lebensgröße
ROCK GIGANTEN
LED ZEPPELIN
„Dallas"-VICTORIA ★ BEATLES ★ NICOLE
POSTERS
JUDAS PRIEST ★ TONI MANG
So könnt Ihr Euch näherkommen:
Geheimsprache mit Briefmarken
KIM WILDE
Am 10. 9. live im „Musikladen"
Neuer Aufklärungs-Report:
Junge Liebe '81
13- bis 18jährige schildern ihre Sex-Erlebnisse

3 ~ CATCH AS CATCH CAN

House Of Salome/Back Street Joe/Stay Awhile/Love Blonde/Dream Sequence/Dancing In The Dark/Shoot To Disable/Can You Hear It/Sparks/Sing It Out For Love

Produced by Ricky Wilde.

UK: RAK SRAK 1654081 (1983).

26.11.83: **90**

Australia
6.02.84: **97**

Finland
11.83: peaked at no.**1** (3), charted for 22 weeks

Germany
28.11.83: 44-24-25-28-**23**-39-36-32-25-49-37-58-57

Netherlands
19.11.83: 42-**35**-40

Sweden
15.11.83: 31-**17**-21-31-37-46 (bi-weekly)

KIM WILDE

CATCH AS CATCH CAN

NEW ALBUM AND CASSETTE INCLUDES THE SINGLES LOVE BLONDE & DANCING IN THE DARK

AVAILABLE FROM VIRGIN, HMV, OUR PRICE & ALL GOOD RECORD SHOPS

RAK RECORDS

Switzerland
13.11.83: 17-19-**6-6**-8-15-10-12-12-9-11-9-22-22-24-24

Recorded at the RAK Studios in central London, *CATCH AS CATCH CAN* was the third and final album Kim recorded for RAK Records.

Ricky and Marty wrote nine of the ten tracks on the album, the one exception being *Dancing In The Dark*, which Nicky Chinn and Paul Gurvitz composed. As he had with his sister's first two albums, Ricky produced the album.

'I think I have been self-critical of some of our material,' said Kim, 'sometimes too much, but I'm very pleased how this album's tuned out … it's a natural evolution both in music and in my physical appearance, the more sophisticated, and the next album we are recording will confirm this change a little more.'

Three singles from *CATCH AS CATCH CAN* were released as singles in various countries, and all three achieved Top 40 status in at least one country:

- *Love Blonde*
- *Dancing In The Dark*
- *House Of Salome*

However, while *Love Blonde* was reasonably successful, both *Dancing In The Dark* and *House Of Salome* were only minor hits for Kim.

The album itself, although it topped the chart in Finland, struggled in most countries. The album charted at no.6 in Switzerland, no.17 in Sweden, no.23 in Germany and no.35 in the Netherlands. The album could only manage a solitary week at no.90 and no.97 in the UK and Australia, respectively.

CATCH AS CATCH CAN was remastered and reissued in Europe in 2009, with five bonus tracks:

Love Blonde (7" Version)/Back Street Driver/Love Blonde (12" Version)/Dancing In The Dark (Nile Rodgers Remix)/(Instrumental)

Deluxe Edition

Released in Europe in 2020, the Deluxe Edition of *CATCH AS CATCH CAN* comprised 2 x CDs and a DVD:

CD1 Bonus Tracks: *Rain On/Back Street Driver/Love Blonde (7" Version)/Dancing In The Dark (RAK Mix)/Can You Hear It (7" Version)/Love Blonde (Extended Version)/Dancing In The Dark (Nile Rodgers Extended Version)/(Instrumental)/(Full Instrumental)*

July 9, 1983 — 40p

Eurythmics vs **RM** — *ringside report!*

RECORD MIRROR

YAZOO LP!

KIM WILDE

- DONNA SUMMER
- HEAVEN 17
- BLUEBELLS
- NONA HENDRYX
- DOUBLE DUTCH GIRLS

Kim Wilde pic by Eugene Adebari

CD2: *House Of Salome (Rough Mix)/Back Street Joe (Original Mix)/Stay Awhile (Rough Mix)/Dream Sequence (Instrumental Demo)/Dancing In The Dark (Rough Mix)/Shoot To Disable (Rough Mix)/Can You Hear It (Rough Mix)/Sparks (Rough Mix)/Sing It Out For Love (Rough Mix)/Sail On (Original Version)/Shoot To Disable (Original Mix)/House Of Salome (Instrumental)/Dream Sequence (In Reverse)/Love Blonde (Popfidelity Allstars Special Remix)/Sparks (Extended Edit)/Can You Hear It (Project K: Project Kim)/Love Blonde (Popfidelity Allstars Instrumental)*

DVD: *Love Blonde/Dancing In The Dark/Love Blonde (Top Of The Pops 1st Performance)/(Top Of The Pops 2nd Performance)/Dancing In The Dark (Harty)/(Crackerjack)/The Very Best Of Kim Wilde (1984 TV Advert)*

At the same time, the original album was reissued on blue vinyl.

nercredi sur 2
6f
salut!
ES DECLARATIONS DE
KIM WILDE
2 SUPER POSTERS
ICHAEL JACKSON RUSTY JAMES
RUSTY JAMES
XCLUSIF!
ANTHONY
DELON
ETABLIT
A VERITE
AKIE QUARTZ
MES PROJETS
OUR 1984"
LEXANDRONI
NE SURPRISE POUR L'ETE
2611 - 220 - 6 F

4 ~ THE VERY BEST OF KIM WILDE

Kids In America/Chequered Love/Water On Glass/2-6-5-8-0/Boys/Our Town/Everything We Know/You'll Never Be So Wrong/Cambodia/View From A Bridge/Love Blonde/House Of Salome/Dancing In The Dark/Child Come Away/Take Me Tonight/Stay Awhile

Japan Bonus Track: *Bitter Is Better.*

UK: RAK WILDE 1 (1984).

18.05.85: 97-93-**78**-96

Australia
27.08.84: peaked at no.**13**, charted for 16 weeks

Germany
20.08.84: **61**

Switzerland
22.07.84: **25**-28-x-28

It's not unusual, when an artist leaves one record label for another, for the first record label to put out a compilation album, and that's exactly what happened when Kim left RAK Records.

Kim and her family had no involvement with what was her first compilation, *THE VERY BEST OF KIM WILDE*.

'I really hated the picture on the cover,' she said, 'the lack of thought behind it, that it actually contained several LP tracks, and I've never really forgiven EMI (RAK's parent company) for it.'

THE VERY BEST OF KIM WILDE achieved no.13 in Australia and no.25 in Switzerland, but was only a minor no.61 and no.78 hit in Germany and the UK, respectively, and the compilation failed to chart at all in most countries.

KIM WILDE
TEASES & DARES
AT OUR PRICE

ALBUM OR CASSETTE ONLY £4.79

KIM WILDE – 'TEASES & DARES'
INCLUDES HER HIT SINGLE 'THE SECOND TIME'

MUSIC, SERVICE, SELECTION – THINK OUR PRICE

COMING SOON: EURYTHMICS · NICK KERSHAW · JAPAN · DURAN DURAN

OUR PRICE Records

MUSIC VIDEOS NOW AVAILABLE AT SELECTED OUR PRICE SHOPS

ADDRESSES

PHONE 01-937 4174 FOR THE ADDRESS OF YOUR LOCAL OUR PRICE RECORD SHOP

5 ~ TEASES & DARES

The Touch/Is It Over/Suburbs Of Moscow/Fit In/Rage To Love/The Second Time/ Bladerunner/Janine/Shangri-La/Thought It Was Goodbye

Produced by Ricky, Marty & Kim Wilde.

UK: MCA Records WILDE 1 (1984).

17.11.84: **66**-79

Finland
11.84: peaked at no.**24**, charted for 3 weeks

Germany
19.11.84: 47-39-**22**-28-38-47-43-36-39-53-47-50-46-38-38-54-63-52-57-55-54-64

Sweden
23.11.84: 39-50-x-x-x-47-x-**35**-x-50 (bi-weekly)

Switzerland
2.12.84: **10**-13-13-14-21-21-25-26-30

USA
2.03.85: 87-**84**-84

Explaining the delay between her third and fourth albums, Kim said, 'First, I changed record company, which wasn't easy due to the complicated contracts. And second, I worked on my own songs, two of which will be heard on the new album. They are the first real original compositions of my career.'

Having decided not to re-sign with RAK Records, Kim signed with MCA Records in 1984. She chose MCA because, 'They offered us such conditions that it was hard to resist them. They left us a lot more freedom than usual to do this work.'

Kim recorded the album that became *TEASES & DARES* at the family's new Select Sound Studios in Knebworth, Hertfordshire.

'We've got our own studio now,' said Kim, 'and lots of time to do things properly. We needed a new start, a fresh input, because the problem over the last year or so has just been a lack of good songs.'

TEASES & DARES, for the first time, featured songs Kim had composed or co-written herself.

'On *TEASES & DARES* I was directly involved in writing three tracks,' she said. 'I am very proud of it, even if the result is far from perfect. I plan to work a lot in 1985 to improve and enrich my writing.'

The songs in question were *Fit In* and *Shangri-La*, which Kim composed herself, and she co-wrote *Thought It Was Goodbye* with her brother and father. The remaining seven tracks on the album were composed by Ricky and Marty.

Another first saw Kim, as well as Marty, credited as co-producing the album with Ricky. 'From design to mixing, we work in perfect harmony,' she said, 'but we are not clinging to each other to the point of choking us.'

The album produced three Top 40 singles:

- *The Second Time* (re-titled *Go For It* in North America)
- *The Touch*
- *Rage To Love*

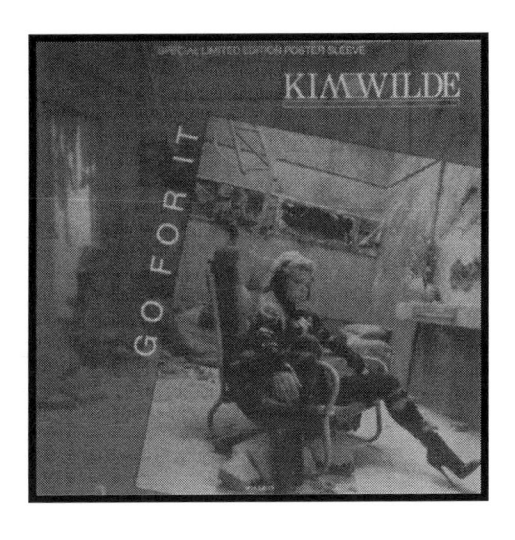

KIM WILDE

Teases & Dares her new album featuring the hit single "The Second Time"

MCA RECORDS

on record and cassette

Although not a single, Kim personal favourite song on the album was *Suburbs Of Moscow*.

'It's about the life of young people in Eastern Europe,' she said, 'being in a cultural conflict on a daily basis. They are living in a dictatorial regime, which doesn't leave any space for personal development, but the jeans they wear show a bond with the Western world.'

TEASES & DARES charted at no.10 in Switzerland, no.22 in Germany, no.24 in Finland and no.35 in Sweden. Sales elsewhere were disappointing, and the album struggled to no.66 in the UK and no.84 in the United States, and it missed the charts altogether in many countries.

TEASES & DARES was remastered and reissued in the UK in 2010, with seven bonus tracks and a bonus CD:

CD1 Bonus Tracks: *Lovers On A Beach/Shangri-La (Alternative Version)/Putty In Your Hands/Turn It On/The Second Time (7" Version)/The Touch (7" Version)/Rage To Love (7" Version)*

Bonus CD: *The Second Time (12" Version)/Lovers On A Beach (12" Version)/Go For It (Extended Dance Version)/The Touch (12" Version)/Shangri-La (12" Version)/Go For It (Dub Version)/Rage To Love (12" Version)/Shanri-La (Special Remix)/The Second Time (US Remix)*

KIM WILDE
THE BIG ALBUM
ANOTHER STEP
FEATURES THE GIANT SINGLE
YOU KEEP ME HANGIN' ON
MCA RECORDS

6 ~ ANOTHER STEP

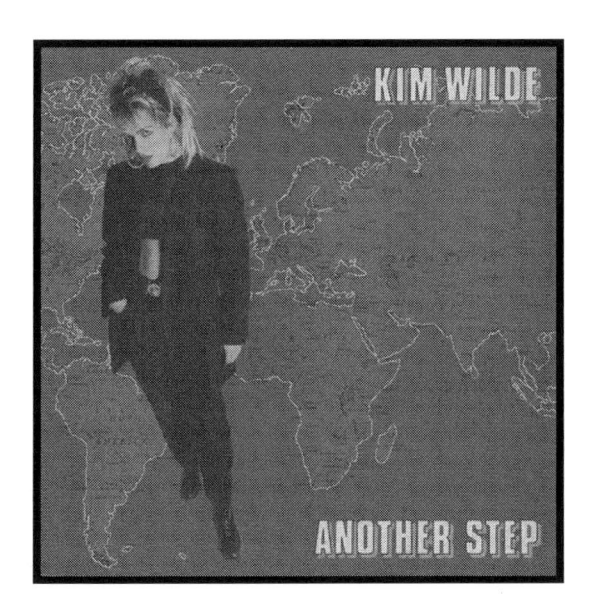

You Keep Me Hangin' On/Hit Him/Another Step (Closer To You)/The Thrill Of It/I've Got So Much Love/Victim/Schoolgirl/Say You Really Want Me/She Hasn't Got Time For You/ Brothers/Missing/How Do You Want My Love/Don't Say Nothing's Changed

Victim only featured on the cassette and CD versions of the album.

Produced by Ricky Wilde, Rod Temperton & Bruce Swedien.

UK: MCA Records MCF 3339 (1986).

15.11.86: 90-88-93
26.09.87: **73**-89

Australia
12.01.87: peaked at no.**31**, charted for 19 weeks

Germany
3.11.86: 61-61-62-63-64-61-63-60-49-48-42-42-**41**-47-51-54-61

Japan
25.10.87: peaked at no.**83**, charted for 3 weeks

Netherlands
7.02.87: **70**

Norway
24.01.87: 16-6-5-3-3-**2**-3-4-4-7-9-12-15-15-16-20

Sweden
22.10.86: **49-49** (bi-weekly)

Switzerland
25.01.87: 7-7-**5-5**-12-22-22-26

USA
2.05.87: 65-60-52-49-44-42-**40-40**-50-52-48-65-70-59-66-76-83-87

Kim's fifth studio album, as well as the family's Select Sound Studio, was also recorded at two studios in Los Angeles, Larrabee Sound Studios and Westlake Recording Studios.

'We were very well prepared for this album,' said Kim, 'and I have been working very hard at it. We managed to choose the twelve strongest works because there was an excess of material.'

The album featured Kim's first duet and her first cover, and the cassette and CD editions of the album featured a thirteenth track – *Victim* – not found on the vinyl release. Notably, including *Victim*, Kim had a hand in writing nine of the 13 tracks on the album. She composed *Don't Say Nothing's Changes* herself, plus co-wrote four tracks with Ricky and Marty, one with Ricky alone, and three with Steve Byrd.

The three tracks Kim didn't write or co-write were her cover of *You Keep Me Hangin' On*, a Holland-Dozier-Holland composition, O.S. Blandamer's *Hit Him* and *Say You Really Want Me*, which Danny Sembello, Donnell Spencer, Jr. and Richard Rudolph wrote for the 1986 film, *Running Scared*. The latter is the song Kim flew to Los Angeles to record.

Four singles, including Kim's first and only chart topper in the United States, were released from ANOTHER STEP:

- *Schoolgirl*
- *You Keep Me Hangin' On*
- *Another Step (Closer To You)*
- *Say You Really Want Me*

ANOTHER STEP, despite the inclusion of *You Keep Me Hangin' On*, failed to live up to Kim's expectations. The album achieved no.2 in Norway, no.5 in Switzerland, no.31 in Australia, no.40 in the United States, no.41 in Germany and no.49 in Sweden, but it was only a minor hit in Japan, the Netherlands and the UK.

TURN BACK THE CLOCK

Shattered Dreams/Heart Of Gold/Turn Back The Clock/Don't Say It's Love/What Other Reason/I Don't Want To Be A Hero/Listen/Different Seasons/Don't Let It End This Way/Foolish Heart

Produced by Calvin Hayes, Mike Nocito & Phil Thornalley.

UK: Virgin V2475 (1988).

23.01.88: **1**-2-3-7-5-6-6-8-8-11-10-14-10-18-21-29-35-50-47-50-52-65-94-97-76-78-74-78-86-65-12-10-14-23-28-42-51-60-91

Pos	LW	Title, Artist		Peak Pos	WoC
1	New	**TURN BACK THE CLOCK** JOHNNY HATES JAZZ	VIRGIN	1	1
2	1 ↓	**POPPED IN SOULED OUT** WET WET WET	PRECIOUS ORGANISATION	1	17
3	4 ↑	**INTRODUCING THE HARDLINE ACCORDING TO ...** TERENCE TRENT D'ARBY	CBS	1	27
4	8 ↑	**THE CHRISTIANS** THE CHRISTIANS	ISLAND	2	13
5	2 ↓	**BAD** MICHAEL JACKSON	EPIC	1	20

Austria
15.02.88: 25-24-**20**-27 (bi-weekly)

Germany
25.01.88: 30-8-6-**5**-8-8-9-9-9-22-23-18-21-14-14-25-29-37-38-45-46-49-59-51-62

Netherlands
23.01.88: 30-**3-3**-4-4-5-8-9-11-18-15-17-22-23-30-32-29-37-62

New Zealand
20.03.88: 40-19-**3-3-3-3**-4-5-10-13-22-27-32-20-x-39-47-39

Norway
16.01.88: 4-2-**1-1**-2-2-5-6-6-6-14-14-18

#	LW		Artist / Title	W
1	2	^	**Johnny Hates Jazz** — Turn Back The Clock	3
2	1	v	**T'Pau** — Bridge Of Spies	9
3	5	^	**Belinda Carlisle** — Heaven On Earth	3
4	3	v	**Jørn Hoel** — Varme ut av is	15
5	6	^	**Foreigner** — Inside Information	7

VG Lista - Album Top 40 — 05/1988

Switzerland
24.01.88: 5-19-5-**4**-7-8-8-14-15-20-30-x-25-x-27

USA
30.04.88: 100-74-65-57-57-60-**56**-60-58-66-73-79

Sweden
20.01.88: 3-**1**-2-3-8-12-20-44 (bi-weekly)

#	LW	Artist / Title	Label / Company	Prefix Suffix	W
1	3	Johnny Hates Jazz / Turn Back The Clock	Virgin / Electra	208676	2
2	NEW	Orup / Orup	WEA / WEA	242264-1	1
3	6	Belinda Carlisle / Heaven On Earth	Virgin / Electra	208824	2
4	1	Agnetha Fältskog / I Stand Alone	WEA / WEA	242231-1	5
5	2	Rick Astley / Whenever You Need Somebody	RCA / Electra	PL 71529	6

Kim, along with Miriam Stockley and Stevie Lange, sang backing vocals on Johnny Hates Jazz's debut album, *TURN BACK THE CLOCK*. The album produced four Top 40 singles:

- *Shattered Dreams*
- *I Don't Want To Be A Hero*
- *Turn Back The Clock*
- *Heart Of Gold*

TURN BACK THE CLOCK topped the chart in Norway, Sweden and the UK, and charted at no.3 in the Netherlands and New Zealand, no.5 in Germany and no.20 in Austria.

KIM WILDE

イイ女。見つめていたい。

全世界で大ヒットとなった「キープ・ミー・ハンギン・オン」から約2年、今や世界のスーパー・スターとなったキム・ワイルドの最新アルバム!!

NEW ALBUM ◎好評発売中

CLOSE

★先着5万名様にサイン入ポートレイト・セット(A〜3、4枚入)をプレゼント!

●プロデュース: リッキー・ワイルド&ニース・ウェイン
●CD:25P2-2161 ¥2,550 ●LP:25P1-2161 ¥2,300 ●CT:25P4-2161 ¥2,300 ●歌詞対訳付

★大ヒット・シングル「YOU CAME」収録

MCA RECORDS

NEW PRICE
CD ¥2,500
LP ¥2,300

ワーナー・パイオニア株式会社

7 ~ CLOSE

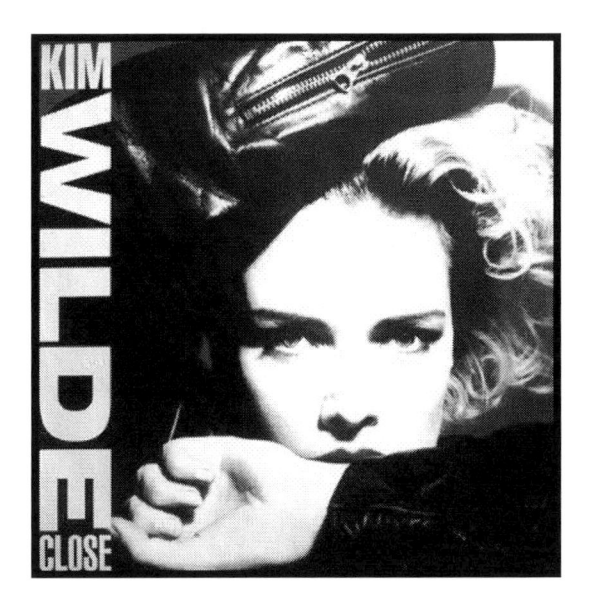

Hey Mister Heartache/You Came/Four Letter Word/Love In The Natural Way/Love's A No/Never Trust A Stranger/You'll Be The One Who'll Lose/European Soul/Stone/Lucky Guy

CD Bonus Track: *Hey Mister Heartache (12" Version)*.

Produced by Ricky Wilde & Tony Swain.

UK: MCA Records MCG 6030 (1988).

25.06.88: 70-98-x-x-95-73-59-46-44-50-60-68-86-x-x-x-71-60-58-61-70-79-90-x-89-x-91-75-55-30-22-14-**8**-12-16-26-29-27-34-29-31-31-44-44-59

Australia
15.08.88: peaked at no.**82**, charted for 11 weeks

Austria
1.10.88: 18-11-26-20-20-18-16-**7**-8-8-9-15-19-20-22 (bi-weekly)

Finland
07.88: peaked at no.**14**, charted for 24 weeks

France
12.02.89: 27-30-26-25-**19**-29-46-50 (bi-weekly)

Germany
20.06.88: 59-47-15-21-24-24-26-28-21-17-16-14-**10**-13-15-18-20-25-27-27-33-32-31-31-32-37-42-45-48-54-53-59-59-60

Italy
12.11.88: **23**

Japan
25.09.88: peaked at no.**38**, charted for 9 weeks

Netherlands
25.06.88: 54-47-69
20.08.88: 70-50-49-43-44
18.02.89: 10-11-11-9-**8**-9-10-11-15-23-25-33-38-49-56-89-95

Norway
18.06.88: 11-7-**6-6**-8-10-9-10-13-14-14-11-13-18-15

Sweden
22.06.88: 12-13-14-18-14-**11**-13-19-29-31-x-19-19-14-12-16-32 (bi-weekly)

Switzerland
10.07.88: **8**-12-11-19-23-15-17-21-10-**8**-10-11-13-12-12-21-15-13-16-16-20-18-23-16-13-13-10-17-15-12-24-19-29-20-20-x-25

Kim recorded her sixth studio album, *CLOSE*, at the family's Select Sound Studios.

'We stayed three months in the studio,' said Kim, 'including mixing, which is very short. We have eliminated a maximum of titles to keep a unity to the album that could be called pop-soul.'

Kim co-wrote eight of the ten songs on the album with a combination of Ricky, Marty and Steve Byrd. The two exceptions were *Four Letter Word*, which Ricky and Marty composed, and a cover of Todd Rundgren's *Lucky Guy*.

'Todd is an extraordinary musician,' said Kim, 'one of the best American rock talents of the last twenty years.'

Kim felt '*CLOSE* truly reflects my musical roots, who are the Beach Boys 'Pet Sound', and then Joni Mitchell and Simon & Garfunkel. Between the lines, we can find my current tastes, from Prefab Sprout to the Christians.'

The album produced five hit singles:

- *Hey Mister Heartache*
- *You Came*
- *Never Trust A Stranger*

- *Four Letter Word*
- *Love In The Natural Way*

Sales of *CLOSE* were undoubtedly boosted by Kim's support of Michael Jackson, on the European leg of his hugely successful Bad Tour.

'When the possibility of supporting Michael Jackson first arose,' said Kim, 'it was something I didn't dare think about. My first reaction was "I can't", to which my mum replied "Why on Earth not?" "But I can't!", I screamed, he's the greatest performer on Earth, he's in a different league!"'

But, encouraged by her family, Kim finally agreed. At the same time, she acknowledged people would be coming to the concerts to see Michael Jackson, not her – but, by the end of her time as Michael's support act, Kim had been seen by over two million people.

'I would never have reached such an amount of people alone,' she said.

CLOSE gave Kim only her second Top 10 album in the UK, after her debut, rising to no.8. The album also gave Kim her first and only Top 40 success in the United States, albeit only just. Elsewhere, the album achieved n.6 in Norway, no.7 in Austria, no.8 in the Netherlands and Switzerland, no.10 in Germany, no.11 in Sweden, no.14 in Finland, no.19 in France, no.23 in Italy and no.38 in Japan.

25th Anniversary Edition

The 25th anniversary of the release of *CLOSE* was celebrated in 2013 with a 2 x CD edition, featuring 21 bonus tracks in total.

CD1 Bonus Tracks: *Tell Me Where You Are/Wotcha Gonna Do/She Hasn't Got Time For You '88/Hey Mister Heartache (Single Version)/You Came (Single Version)/Never Trust A Stranger (Single Version)/Love In The Natural Way (Video Edit)/You Came (Shep Pettibone US Single Version)*

Bonus CD: *Hey Mister Heartache (12" Version)/(Kilo Watt Remix)/(Bonus Beats)/ (Acapella With Percussion)/You Came (12" Version)/(Shep Pettibone 12" Mix)/(Dub Version #1)/(Dub Version #2)/Never Trust A Stranger (12" Version)/(Sanjazz Mix)/Four Letter Word (12" Version)/(Late Night Mix)/Love In The Natural Way (Extended Version)*

ΠΟΠ ΚΟΡΝ

ΟΚΤΩΒΡΙΟΣ 1988
Μηνιαίο Μουσικό Περιοδικό • Τεύχος 42 • Δρχ. 350

SUPER POSTER: EUROPE + POSTER: BON JOVI

KIM WILDE

ΚΙ ΑΚΟΜΗ: ΣΥΝΕΝΤΕΥΞΗ ΜΕ ΤΟΝ MORTEN ΤΩΝ A.HA
NICK KAMEN + PET SHOP BOYS + ELTON JOHN + LEVEL 42 + SPAGNA
BLOW MONKEYS + SMITHS + DEAD OR ALIVE + BOMB THE BASS
WET WET WET ENANTION BROS

8 ~ LOVE MOVES

It's Here/Love (Send Him Back To Me)/Storm In Our Hearts/World In Perfect Harmony/ Someday/Time/Who's To Blame/Can't Get Enough (Of Your Love)/In Hollywood/I Can't Say Goodbye

Produced by Ricky Wilde.

UK: MCA Records MCG 6088 (1990).

26.05.90: **37**-50-62

Finland
05.90: peaked at no.**18**, charted for 7 weeks

France
21.06.90: 40-25-27-**19**-26-23-**19**-23-45

Germany
11.06.90: 41-49-**24**-26-32-36-39-51-55-58-56-70-76-83-86

Japan
10.07.90: **88**

Netherlands
9.06.90: 74-59-**39**-**39**-55-68-77-92

Norway
2.06.90: 12-**10**-12-12-18-20

Sweden
6.06.90: **10**-14-25 (bi-weekly)

Switzerland
3.06.90: 15-17-**12-12**-23-30-24-x-31-x-39

Kim co-wrote six of the ten songs she recorded for her seventh studio with album with her brother, Ricky. The remaining four tracks, namely *Love (Send Her Back To Me)*, *Storm In Our Hearts*, *Who's To Blame* and *In Hollywood*, were composed by Tony Swain. For the first time on one of his daughter's albums, Marty was notable by his absence from the song-writing credits on *LOVE MOVES*.

'There are so many different atmospheres on the record,' said Kim, 'it's almost like a trip. This record is totally me. Every contradiction within me, I can find on *LOVE MOVES*. I can't live without contradictions. When they're not, I will create them if I have to.'

Five singles were released from *LOVE MOVES* in various countries, but only two of them achieved Top 40 status anywhere:

- *It's Here*
- *Can't Get Enough (Of Your Love)*

I Can't Say Goodbye and *Time* were both minor hits in the UK, peaking at no.51 and no.71, respectfully, while the fifth single *World In Perfect Harmony* failed to chart anywhere.

LOVE MOVES failed to match the success of *CLOSE*, charting at no.10 in Norway and Sweden, no.12 in Switzerland, no.18 in Finland, no.19 in France, no.24 in Germany, no.37 in the UK and no.39 in the Netherlands.

'It was a very strong album,' said Kim, 'and it was disappointing that it didn't do well. But it didn't really come as too much of a surprise, because my career before then had always been very up and down – so it wasn't a complete shock.'

9 ~ LOVE IS

Love Is Holy/Who Do You Think You Are?/I Believe In You/Touched By Your Magic/I Won't Change The Way That I Feel/Million Miles Away/The Light Of The Moon (Belongs To Me)/Heart Over Mind/A Miracle's Coming/Try Again/Too Late

Produced by Ricky Wilde, except *Love Is Holy*, *I Won't Change The Way That I Feel* and *A Miracle's Coming*, which Rick Nowels produced.

UK: MCA Records MCA 10625 (1992).

30.05.92: **21**-37-63

Australia
20.07.92: peaked at no.**95**, charted for 2 weeks

Austria
14.06.92: 38-**22**-28-23-32-27-33-35-39-36-36

Germany
15.06.92: 50-73-**42**-46-53-63-68-73-76-77-81-76-84

Japan
22.07.92: peaked at no.**42**, charted for 6 weeks

Netherlands
30.05.92: 84-69-58-**53**-58-69-82

Sweden
10.06.92: **25**-44 (bi-weekly)

Switzerland
31.05.92: 26-13-11-7-8-15-10-12-12-16-23-31-23-36-31

Kim co-wrote seven of the eleven tracks she recorded for her *LOVE IS* album, with either her brother Ricky, Rick Nowels or Steve Byrd. Ricky co-wrote *I Believe In You* and *Touched By Your Magic* with Mick Silver, Ellen Shipley and Rick Nowels wrote *Love Is Holy*, and Andy Stewart, David Munday, John Hall and Nick Whitecross were responsible for *Too Late*.

'For the first time ever I didn't want to change a single thing,' said Kim. 'Making the album was a long and gradual process, and it took me two years to complete it. The only challenge was to defeat my fear of writing songs.'

Four singles were released from *LOVE IS* in various countries, but only two of them achieved Top 40 status anywhere:

- *Love Is Holy*
- *Heart Over Mind*

Who Do You Think You Are was a minor hit in Germany, the Netherlands and the UK, but the final single *Million Miles Away* failed to chart anywhere.

LOVE IS was moderately successful, and achieved no.7 in Switzerland, no.21 in the UK, no.22 in Austria, no.25 in Sweden, and no.42 in Germany and Japan.

KIM WILDE
THE SINGLES COLLECTION 1981 – 1993

Kids in America • Chequered Love •
Another Step • Cambodia •
Never Trust A Stranger •
Love Is Holy • Love Blond •
If I Can't Have You •
You Keep Me Hangin' On • You Came •
Four Letter Word • View From A Bridge •
Rage To Love • The Second Time •
Child Come Away • In My Life

Kim Wilde, The Singles Collection 1981-1993

Nu overal verkrijgbaar op Compact disc en Cassette

MCA   BMG

10 ~ THE SINGLES COLLECTION 1981-1993

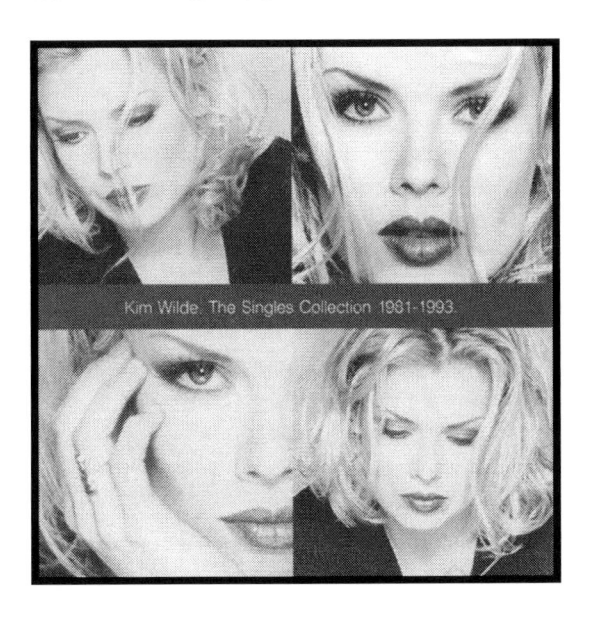

Kids In America/Chequered Love/Water On Glass/Cambodia (Single Version)/View From A Bridge/Child Come Away/Love Blonde/The Second Time/Rage To Love/You Keep Me Hangin' On/Another Step (Closer To You) (7" Remix)/You Came (7" Version)/Never Trust A Stranger (Single Mix)/Four Letter Word/Love Is Holy/If I Can't Have You/In My Life

UK: MCA Records MCA 10921 (1993).

25.09.93: **11-11**-14-20-31-51-64

Australia
11.10.93: peaked at no.**6**, charted for 21 weeks

Austria
3.10.93: **26-26-26**-30

Finland
09.93: peaked at no.**5**, charted for 15 weeks

Germany
27.09.93: 83-47-**21**-27-24-30-32-45-59-65-70-73-80

Japan
21.10.93: peaked at no.**21**, charted for 6 weeks

Netherlands
18.09.93: 87-71-45-22-7-6-**5**-6-6-8-9-11-15-15-26-43-45-34-31-42-52-81-87-85-81-72-70-71-100

Sweden
22.09.93: 26-32-32-19-13-**11**-19-23-42-43

Switzerland
8.10.93: 23-30-20-20-**18**-27-30-39-34-x-24

Although her first record company RAK Records released *THE VERY BEST OF KIM WILDE* after she switched labels, Kim had no say about any aspect the album, so *THE SINGLES COLLECTION 1981-1993* was the first 'greatest hits' compilation she was involved with.

'It's an important year for me,' she said. 'My whole thirteen year career is on one CD – that's very special.'

Kim was determined to support and promote the compilation with a hit single, but finding the right song proved a real challenge.

'If we'd felt that we had the song that could have been a hit,' she said, 'we'd have been overjoyed. But we didn't think we had, especially after the last two singles not doing very well at all. So we thought, sod it! We're gonna do a bloody good cover!'

The cover Kim eventually settled on was the Yvonne Elliman hit, *If I Can't Have You*, which the Bee Gees wrote for the movie, *Saturday Night Fever*. *If I Can't Have You* duly gave Kim her biggest hit for some years in many countries.

The compilation also featured another new song, *In My Life*, which Kim co-wrote with Ricky. *In My Life* was also issued as a single, as the follow-up to *If I Can't Have You*, and it was a minor hit in Australia, Germany and the UK, but it failed to achieve Top 40 status anywhere.

THE SINGLES COLLECTION 1981-1993 charted at no.5 in Finland and the Netherlands, no.6 in Australia, no.11 in the UK, no.18 in Switzerland, no.21 in Germany and Japan, and no.26 in Austria.

The compilation was accompanied by a home music video, which featured 12 of Kim's promos.

11 ~ NOW & FOREVER

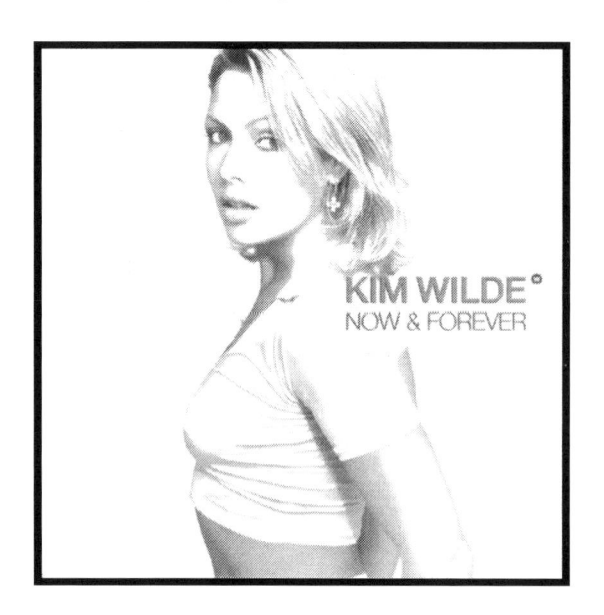

Breakin' Away/High On You/This I Swear/C'mon Love Me/True To You/Hypnotise/ Heaven/Sweet Inspiration/Where Do You Go From Here/Hold On/You're All I Wanna Do/Life & Soul/Now & Forever/Back To Heaven

Japan Bonus Track: *Staying With My Baby*.

Produced by Ricky Wilde, C.J. Mackintosh & Serious Rope.

UK: MCA Records MCD 60002 (1995).

NOW & FOREVER wasn't a hit in the UK.

Switzerland
12.11.95: **37**-x-39

NOW & FOREVER was Kim's ninth studio album, and she felt it was time to leave her past behind, and choose a different direction.

'My new CD has become a dance/R&B/soul record,' she said. 'I was listening to a lot of records – Aaliyah, S.W.V., Mary J. Blige, that sort of thing. I wanted very much to make such a record myself. I have always been a big fan of soul ever since I was a child. I loved Aretha Franklin, Chaka Khan and Stevie Wonder. For the first time, I've come out to show my soul roots.'

As well as her brother Ricky, Kim worked on the album with C.J Mackintosh and the Serious Rope team. But the change in direction didn't please the majority of Kim's fans. Only two singles were released from the album:

- *Breakin' Away*
- *This I Swear*

The singles charted at no.43 and no.46 in the UK, respectfully, but neither achieved Top 40 status anywhere.

NOW & FOREVER became Kim's first album to fail to enter the chart in the UK. The only country where the album did chart was Switzerland, where it spent two non-consecutive weeks on the chart, peaking at no.37.

During the *NOW & FORVER* sessions, Kim recorded a cover of Evelyn 'Champagne' King's disco classic, *Shame*, which was a hit in 1977-78. Although Kim's version failed to make the album, the track was remixed, and released as the follow-up to *This I Swear*, but it failed to chart anywhere.

Following the release of *NOW & FOREVER*, Kim started working on the musical, *Tommy*, and here she met co-star Hal Fowler. The couple married on 1st September 1996, and their first child Harry Tristan was born 16 months later.

Wanting to focus on her family, and her second career in horticulture, Kim quietly retired from the music scene, and it would be over a decade before she released her tenth studio album.

Hertfordshire

£2.00

Issue 12 — February 2001

YOUR LIVELY COUNTY MAGAZINE

Auctions are lots of fun

Chocolate secrets

spotlight on Ware

Kim Wilde

Laurence Llewelyn-Bowen

Joanna Lumley

butlers secrets

12 ~ THE VERY BEST OF KIM WILDE

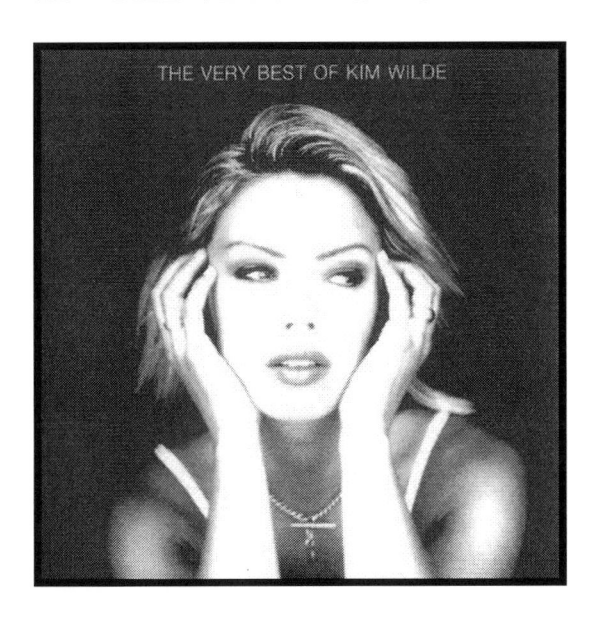

Kids In America/Chequered Love/Water On Glass/Cambodia/View From A Bridge/Child Come Away/Love Blonde/Rage To Love/You Keep Me Hangin' On/Another Step (Closer To You)/You Came/Never Trust A Stranger/Four Letter Word/If I Can't Have You/Loved/ View From A Bridge (Raw Remix/Edit)/Kids In America (D-Bop's Bright Lights Mix/Edit)

UK: EMI 7243 5 35957 2 2 (2001).

THE VERY BEST OF KIM WILDE wasn't a hit in the UK.

Finland
2.02.02: 26-**23**-29

Sweden
1.02.02: 27-**20**-33-31-44

With Kim focussing on her family and her interest in horticulture, another greatest hits package was almost inevitable.

Kim's second compilation titled *THE VERY BEST OF KIM WILDE* did at least have her approval, but the track listing was very similar to 1993's *THE SINGLES COLLECTION 1981-1993*. As well as 15 hits, the new album featured two remixes and one previously unreleased song, *Loved*, which was a Top 40 hit in several countries.

Predictably, *THE VERY BEST OF KIM WILDE* failed to match the success of *THE SINGLES COLLECTION 1981-1993*, but it did achieve no.20 in Sweden and no.23 in Finland. The compilation was also a very minor no.164 hit in the UK, but it missed the chart in most countries.

13 ~ NEVER SAY NEVER

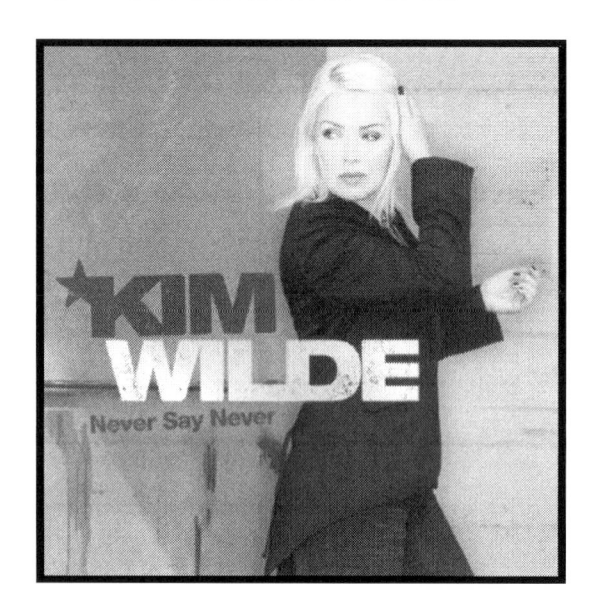

Perfect Girl/You Came (2006 Version)/Together We Belong/Forgive Me/Four Letter Word (2006 Version)/You Keep Me Hangin' On (2006 Version)/Baby Obey Me/Kids In America (2006 Version)/I Fly/Game Over/Lost Without You/View From A Bridge (2006 Version)/ Maybe I'm Crazy/Cambodia (Paul Oakenfold Remix)

Bonus DVD (Deluxe Edition): *You Came (Music Video)/(Alternate Music Video – 'In Bed With Kim Wilde')/(Groovenut Short Edit)/*A Date With Kim Wilde: The Never Say Never Interview/Biography/Photo Gallery

Produced by Ricky Wilde & Uwe Fahrenkrog-Petersen.

UK: Not Released.

Europe: EMI 00946 3 71863 2 9 (2006).

Austria
22.09.06: **22**-30-39-58-71

Belgium
23.09.06: 40-**32**-36-38-38-47-70-89

Finland
21.09.06: **30**-32-40

France
23.09.06: 27-49-**22**-31-39-44-68-96

Germany
22.09.06: **17**-33-38-48-56-72-95

Netherlands
16.09.06: **32**-38-49-58-61-64-68-87

Switzerland
24.09.06: **11**-15-19-33-35-43-46-54-87

When she married, started a family and embarked on a second career in horticulture, Kim admits she was disillusioned with the music business, and she had no plans to make any sort of a comeback.

'There were a few times in my career,' she said, 'a few times in my life really, when I was saying "I'll never do that, I'll never go back into the industry, I'll never do an '80s retro thing, I'll never make a comeback" … But after doing the '80s tours and really loving it, enjoying it and being quite good at it really, I thought actually saying "Never" is really dull, and you should never say never, because life has a way of surprising you sometimes.'

Kim signed a new record deal with the German division of EMI in 2005, and worked on her first new album for over a decade with a former member of the German band Nena, Uwe Fahrenkrog-Petersen. The resultant 14 tracks album *NEVER SAY NEVER* featured up-dated versions of six of Kim's biggest hits, together with eight new songs, three of which Kim co-wrote, namely *Together We Belong*, *Forgive Me* and *Baby Obey Me*.

You Came 2006 was released as the albums lead single, and returned Kim to the charts in most countries ~ however, like the album, it wasn't issued in the UK.

Three further singles were released from the album:

- *Perfect Girl*
- *Together We Belong*
- *Baby Obey Me*

Perfect Girl was a minor no.52 hit in Germany, but *Together We Belong* and *Baby Obey Me* both failed to chart anywhere. The latter included a remix featuring the German rapper Ill Inspecta.

As well as continental Europe, NEVER SAY NEVER was released in Japan and South Africa, but the album wasn't released in Australasia, North America or the UK. The album was a moderate hit, and achieved no.11 in Switzerland, no.17 in Germany, no.22 in Austria, no.30 in Finland, and no.32 in Belgium and the Netherlands.

14 ~ COME OUT AND PLAY

King Of The World/Lights Down Low/Real Life/Greatest Journey/I Want What I Want/ Love Conquers All/Hey! You!/Suicide/This Paranoia/Loving You More/Get Out/My Wish Is Your Command/Jessica

Produced by Ricky Wilde & Andrew Murray, except Kim co-produced *Jessica*, Stephen Jones co-produced *Suicide*, Dave Thomas, J. & John McLaughlin produced *King Of The World* & *I Want What I Want*, Pete Kirtley & Sacha Collisson produced *Get Out*, Paul Humphries & Philip Larsen produced *Love Conquers All*, Philip Larsen produced *Loving You More*, Carsten Heller produced *Hey! You!*

Digital Bonus Tracks: *Carry Me Home* & *Lights Down Low (Music Video)*.

France Deluxe Edition Bonus Tracks: *Carry Me Home, Addicted To You, Party On The Brink* & *Snakes & Ladders*.

UK: Not Released.

Germany: Columbia SevenOne Music 88697758202 (2010).

10.09.10: **10**-14-15-24-27-34-40-79

Austria
10.09.10: **24**-41-47-60

Switzerland
12.09.10: **9**-16-31-36-49-70-91

Kim was fast approaching her 50th birthday when she released her eleventh studio album, *COME OUT AND PLAY*.

'Come out and play is a line in this song,' said Kim, referring to *Hey! You!*, 'but also the backbone for the entire album, and hence the title of the album … We wanted to bring the old sound into a new century, and I think we did it. And the songs express how I feel now – positive and happy.'

Kim wrote one song on the album, *Jessica*, herself, and she co-wrote seven others; Jessica was the name of the family's seven year old Airedale terrier. The album featured two duets, *Greatest Journey* with Heaven 17's Glenn Gregory, and *Love Conquers All* with Nick Kershaw. The album also featured a guitar solo on one track by someone very special to Kim.

'I wrote the song *This Paranoia* during a journey through Sweden,' said Kim, 'and there was some space for a guitar solo. I thought, "I know someone who's really good at playing guitar!".'

That someone was Kim's twelve year old son, Harry.

'I asked Harry, and it was agreed,' said Kim. 'Now I'd like to take him to a few concerts – you know, proud mums love to show-off their sons!'

COME OUT AND PLAY was only released in Germany, Austria and Switzerland. Two singles were planned from the album:

- *Lights Down Low*
- *Real Life*

Lights Down Low was a Top 40 hit in Germany, however, although a promo CD single was issued in Germany, the full release of *Real Life* was cancelled.

Given its limited release, *COME OUT AND PLAY* sold well, and charted at no.9 in Switzerland, no.10 in Germany and no.24 in Austria.

15 ~ SNAPSHOTS

It's Alright/In Between Days/About You Now/Sleeping Satellite/To France/A Little Respect/Remember Me/Anyone Who Had A Heart/Wonderful Life/They Don't Know/Beautiful Ones/Just What I Needed/Ever Fallen In Love (With Someone You Shouldn't've)/Kooks

Exclusive Edition Bonus Track: *Forever Young.*

iTunes Bonus Tracks: *I'll Stand By You/It's Alright (Music Video)/Sleeping Satellite (Music Video)/Track By Track (Pre-Order Only Music Video).*

Produced by Ricky Wilde & Andrew Murray, except Ricky Wilde produced *Kooks*, Alex Rethwisch produced *In Between Days, About You Now, Sleeping Satellite, They Don't Know & Just What I Needed,* Alex G. produced *It's Alright & A Little Respect.*

UK: Columbia SevenOne Music 886979 41172 (2011).

SNAPSHOTS wasn't a hit in the UK.

Germany
9.09.11: **14**-34-42-71

Switzerland
11.09.11: **27**-50-69

QuoFest 2011

Starring STATUS QUO ROY WOOD KIM WILDE

DECEMBER 2011

SAT	3rd	BIRMINGHAM LG ARENA	0844 338 8000
SUN	4th	SHEFFIELD MOTORPOINT ARENA	0114 256 5656
TUE	6th	LIVERPOOL ECHO ARENA	0844 800 0400
WED	7th	NOTTINGHAM CAPITAL FM ARENA	08444 124 624
FRI	9th	BRIGHTON CENTRE	0844 847 1515
SAT	10th	CARDIFF MOTORPOINT ARENA	02920 224 488
SUN	11th	LONDON O$_2$ ARENA	0844 856 0202
TUE	13th	BOURNEMOUTH BIC	0844 576 3000
WED	14th	PLYMOUTH PAVILIONS	0845 146 1460
FRI	16th	NEWCASTLE METRO RADIO ARENA	0844 493 6666
SAT	17th	GLASGOW SECC	0844 395 4000

BUY ONLINE AT LIVENATION.CO.UK

SNAPSHOTS was Kim's 12th studio album, and her first album of covers – an idea suggested to her by her record company.

'At my shows I always played a lot of cover versions,' she said, 'which are always well received, and the timing for such a covers project is now perfect. I'm 50 years old, with 30 years in the music business, so I can do something special. In addition, the songs are already written, so I have so much less work than usual!'

The album featured a duet with Kim's husband, Hal Fowler, on David Bowie's *Kooks*. Unlike her previous two albums, *SNAPSHOTS* was released in the UK, albeit three months after it was issued in Germany.

'It's a tribute to the pop music that has shaped my life,' said Kim. 'Some songs are very personal to me. *Anyone Who Had A Heart* by Cilla Black, for example, impressed me deeply as a child. Others, like *Beautiful Ones* by Suede, I've chosen because they're great pop songs that I like to sing.'

Three singles were released from *SNAPSHOTS* in Germany. *It's Alright* b/w *Sleeping Satellite* was released as a CD single, while *To France* and *Ever Fallen In Love* b/w the non-album *Spirit In The Sky* were both released digitally. *It's Alright/Sleeping Satellite* sneaked a week at no.98, but the other two singles failed to chart.

SNAPSHOTS charted at no.14 in Germany and no.27 in Switzerland, but it wasn't a hit in the UK.

16 ~ HERE COME THE ALIENS

1969/Pop Don't Stop/Kandy Krush/Stereo Shot/Yours 'Til The End/Solstice/Addicted To You/Birthday/Cyber Nation War/Different Story/Rock The Paradiso/Rosetta

Bonus CD (Deluxe Edition): *Amoureux des Reves/Fight Temptation/Yours 'Til The End (Infinity Mix)/Stereo Shot-1969-A Different Story (Numinous Mix)/Cyber Nation War (Keyboard Warrior Mix)/You Came (Live 2018)/Cambodia (Live 2018)/Kids In America (Live 2018)*

Produced by Ricky Wilde.

UK: Wildeflower Records WFR003CD (2018).

29.03.18: **21**-76

Austria
30.03.18: **34**

Belgium
24.03.18: **48**

Germany
23.03.18: **11**-57-85

Netherlands
24.03.18: **74**

Switzerland
25.03.18: **10**-38-70-83

Kim's most recent studio album was inspired by seeing a UFO in her Hertfordshire back garden in June 2009.

'I was in my garden with a friend,' she said, 'the day after Michael Jackson died (25th June 2009), and we saw two bright lights in the sky. They were about twenty times the size of an aeroplane … it was in the local paper, as we weren't the only ones who saw it.'

The experience had a profound effect on Kim, and made her think that somebody is looking after us.

'I felt connected to the universe,' she said, 'and it's made me really inspired, full of hope and wonder.'

HERE COME THE ALIENS was a real family affair.

'We started writing the album several years ago,' said Kim, 'but then I did a Christmas album (*WILDE WINTER SONGBOOK*), which interrupted things a bit. Then there was lots of live stuff and family stuff, and things got put on the back burner for a while, but now it just seemed like the right time to put it out.'

Kim co-wrote eight of the 12 tracks on the standard edition of *HERE COME THE ALIENS*, and one of the two new songs on the deluxe edition. Her brother Ricky co-wrote 11 of the 12 tracks, plus both of the new songs on the deluxe edition of the album; he also featured alongside Kim on *Pop Don't Stop*. Kim's daughter Roxanne co-wrote one track, *Addicted To You*, while her niece (Ricky's daughter) Scarlett co-wrote four songs, *Pop Don't Stop*, *Stereo Shot*, *Birthday* and *Rock The Paradiso*. Scarlett was also responsible for the album's striking artwork.

Three singles were released from the album, with a fourth being released from the deluxe edition of the album:

- *Pop Don't Stop*

- *Kandy Krush*
- *Birthday*
- *Amoureux des Reves*

All were singles were issued digitally only, although promo CD singles of *Kandy Krush* and *Birthday* were released in the UK, and all four singles failed to chart anywhere.

HERE COME THE ALIENS made its chart debut at no.21 in the UK, making it the first of Kim's albums to enter the Top 100 since 1993, when *THE SINGLES COLLECTION 1981-1993* achieved no.11. Elsewhere, the album charted at no.10 in Switzerland, no.11 in Germany, no.34 in Austria and no.48 in Belgium. The album was also a minor no.74 hit in the Netherlands.

'I was really excited to have an album that was getting played on national radio,' said Kim, 'and being critically acclaimed, and people loving it after all these years. I feel like I've found that bookend I wanted. My career began in a spectacular way, with a great song written by my father and my brother Ricky (*Kids In America*). I wanted to try and balance it, to have the end of my career have the same kind of impact. And it has had a similar impact, and bookended my career – it's a balanced career now.'

Seven months after the standard edition of *HERE COME THE ALIENS* was released, a deluxe edition with a bonus CD was issued, which featured two new songs, three remixes, and live versions of Kim's hits *You Came*, *Cambodia* and *Kids In America*, all recorded in 2018.

17 ~ ALIENS LIVE

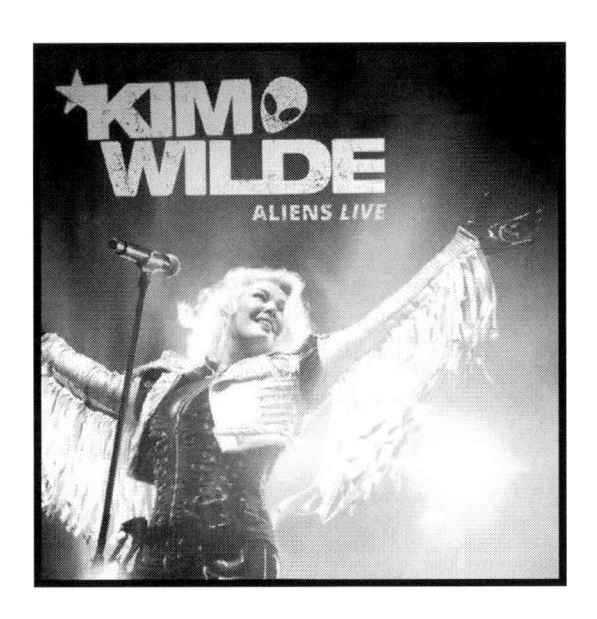

CD1: *Stereo Shot (Live In London)/Water On Glass (Live In Antwerp)/Never Trust A Stranger (Live In Gateshead)/Kandy Krush (Live In Utrecht)/Cambodia (Live In Paris)/Birthday (Live In Munich)/Yours 'Til The End (Live In Hannover)/Solstice (Live In Berlin)/Words Fell Down (Live In Salford)/Bladerunner (Live In Hamburg)*

CD2: *Rosetta (Live In Bochum)/Cyber War Nation (Live In Haarlem)/View From A Bridge (Live In Glasgow)/Chequered Love (Live In Bournemouth)/You Came (Live In Birmingham)/You Keep Me Hangin' On (Live In Vienna)/1969 (Live In Zurich)/Pop Don't Stop (Live In Mannheim)/Kids In America (Live In London)*

Europe: Ear Music 0214066EMU (2019).

ALIENS LIVE wasn't a hit in the UK.

Germany
23.08.19: **40**

Switzerland
25.08.19: **43**

Kim's very first live album – a double – was recorded during her successful Here Come The Aliens Tour, and brought together some of her greatest hits, together with songs from the album that gave the tour its name.

As well as a double CD, *ALIENS LIVE* was released as a limited edition neon orange vinyl double album, with only 250 numbered copies made available in the UK.

KIM
WILDE
HERE COME THE ALIENS
THE TOUR
DIENSTAG
02.10.`18
MÜNCHEN
MUFFATHALLE
BEGINN: 20:00 Uhr
semmel concerts
Telefonischer Kartenservice:
01806 / 57 00 70
PGM
NEUES ALBUM!
Ab dem 16.3. im Handel
TICKETS unter: www.eventim.de

> The **pop icon of the 80s** is celebrating **almost 40 years of performing** with her **first ever live album**
>
> Feat. her biggest hits such as
> **"You Came",**
> **"Kids In America",**
> **"You Keep Me Hangin' On"**
> and **incredible new songs** from her most recent studio album
>
> **Ltd. Neon-Orange 180gr 2LP + Download**

ALIENS LIVE achieved Top 40 status by debuting at no.40 in Germany, before falling off the chart again the following week. The album also spent a solitary week at no.43 in Switzerland, but it wasn't a hit anywhere else.

WEEKBLAD
NR. 399 • 8 NOVEMBER 1981
• 32 BF •
OLIVIA
Liever niet 'live'
ROB DE NIJS
de hel voorbij
THE STONES
razen over Amerika
Sting
Arnold
Olivia
nieuw!!!
POSTERS
KIM WILDE
Jaloerse klikspaan
STING
Bang voor de bom

KIM'S TOP 15 ALBUMS

This Top 15 has been compiled using the same points system as for Kim's Top 25 Singles listing.

Rank/Album/Points

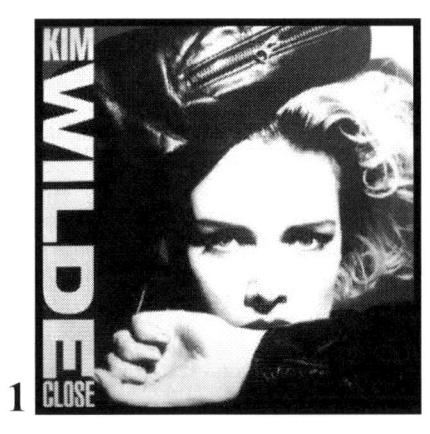

1   *CLOSE* – 1046 points

2   *SELECT* – 851 points

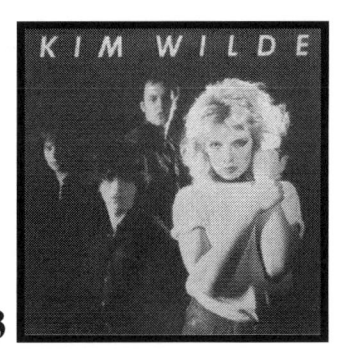

3   *KIM WILDE* – 780 points

Rank/Album/Points

4 *THE SINGLES COLLECTION 1981-1993* – 740 points

5 *LOVE MOVES* – 579 points

6. *ANOTHER STEP* – 476 points
7. *NEVER SAY NEVER* – 463 points
8. *CATCH AS CATCH CAN* – 448 points
9. *LOVE IS* – 431 points
10. *TEASES & DARES* – 319 points

11. *HERE COME THE ALIENS* – 317 points
12. *COME OUT & PLAY* – 229 points
13. *THE VERY BEST OF* (1984) – 184 points
14. *SNAPSHOTS* – 137 points
15. *THE VERY BEST OF* (2001) – 133 points

Kim's 1988 album *CLOSE* emerges as her most successful album, ahead of *SELECT* and her self-titled debut, with *THE SINGLES COLLECTION 1981-1993* and *LOVE MOVES* completing the Top 5.

Kim's most recent album to make the Top 15 is her 2018 album *HERE COME THE ALIENS*, which narrowly fails to make the Top 10 by just two points.

ALBUMS TRIVIA

To date, 17 of Kim's albums have achieved Top 40 albums in one or more of the countries featured in this book.

There follows a country-by-country look at Kim's most successful albums, starting with her homeland.

KIM WILDE IN THE UK

Kim has achieved 11 hit albums in the UK, which spent 90 weeks on the chart.

Her most successful album is *KIM WILDE*, which peaked at no.3.

Albums with the most Top 100 weeks

38 weeks	*CLOSE*
14 weeks	*KIM WILDE*
11 weeks	*SELECT*
7 weeks	*THE SINGLES COLLECTION 1981-1993*
5 weeks	*ANOTHER STEP*

The Brit Certified/BPI (British Phonographic Industry) Awards

The BPI began certifying albums in 1973, and since 1979 the awards have been as follows: Silver = 60,000, Gold = 100,000, Platinum = 300,000. Multi-Platinum awards were introduced in February 1987.

In July 2013 the BPI automated awards, and awards from this date are based on actual sales since February 1994, not shipments.

Platinum	*CLOSE* (October 1989) = 300,000
Gold	*KIM WILDE* (September 1981) = 100,000
Gold	*THE SINGLES COLLECTION 1981-1993* (March 1994) = 100,000
Silver	*SELECT* (May 1982) = 60,000

KIM WILDE IN AUSTRALIA

Kim has achieved nine hit albums in Australia, which spent 98 weeks on the chart.

Her most successful album is *THE SINGLES COLLECTION 1981-1993*, which peaked at no.6.

Albums with the most weeks

21 weeks	*THE SINGLES COLLECTION 1981-1993*
19 weeks	*ANOTHER STEP*
16 weeks	*THE VERY BEST OF KIM WILDE* (1984)
15 weeks	*KIM WILDE*
12 weeks	*SELECT*
11 weeks	*CLOSE*

KIM WILDE IS AUSTRIA

Kim has achieved seven hit albums in Austria, which spent 57 weeks on the chart.

Her most successful album is *CLOSE*, which peaked at no.7.

Albums with the most weeks

30 weeks	*CLOSE*
11 weeks	*LOVE IS*
5 weeks	*NEVER SAY NEVER*
4 weeks	*THE SINGLES COLLECTION 1981-1993*
4 weeks	*COME OUT AND PLAY*

KIM WILDE IN BELGIUM (Flanders)

Since 1995, Kim has achieved two hit albums in Belgium (Flanders), which spent nine weeks on the chart.

Her most successful album is *NEVER SAY NEVER*, which peaked at no.32.

Albums with the most weeks

8 weeks	*NEVER SAY NEVER*
1 week	*HERE COME THE ALIENS*

KIM WILDE IN FINLAND

Kim has achieved nine hit albums in Finland, which spent 123 weeks on the chart.

No.1 Albums

1982   *SELECT*
1983   *CATCH AS CATCH CAN*

Both albums topped the chart for three weeks.

Albums with the most weeks

26 weeks   *SELECT*
24 weeks   *CLOSE*
22 weeks   *CATCH AS CATCH CAN*
20 weeks   *KIM WILDE*
15 weeks   *THE SINGLES COLLECTION 1981-1993*

KIM WILDE IN FRANCE

Kim has achieved three hit albums in France, which spent 42 weeks on the chart.

Her most successful albums are *CLOSE* and *LOVE MOVES*, which both peaked at no.19.

Albums with the most weeks

18 weeks   *LOVE MOVES*
16 weeks   *CLOSE*
 8 weeks   *NEVER SAY NEVER*

KIM WILDE IN GERMANY

Kim has achieved 15 hit albums in Germany, which spent 201 weeks on the chart.

No.1 Albums

1981   *KIM WILDE*

KIM WILDE topped the chart for five weeks.

Albums with the most weeks

34 weeks   *CLOSE*
31 weeks   *KIM WILDE*
22 weeks   *TEASES & DARES*

19 weeks	*SELECT*
17 weeks	*ANOTHER STEP*
15 weeks	*LOVE MOVES*
13 weeks	*CATCH AS CATCH CAN*
13 weeks	*LOVE IS*
13 weeks	*THE SINGLES COLLECTION 1981-1993*

KIM WILDE IN ITALY

Only one of Kim's albums, *CLOSE*, has charted in Italy. It peaked at no.23, and spent a solitary week on the chart.

KIM WILDE IN JAPAN

Kim has achieved seven hit albums in Japan, which spent 42 weeks on the chart.

Her most successful album is *THE SINGLES COLLECTION 1981-1993*, which peaked at no.21.

Albums with the most weeks

13 weeks	*SELECT*
9 weeks	*CLOSE*
6 weeks	*LOVE IS*
6 weeks	*THE SINGLES COLLECTION 1981-1993*
4 weeks	*KIM WILDE*

KIM WILDE IN THE NETHERLANDS

Kim has achieved 10 hit albums in the Netherlands, which spent 107 weeks on the chart.

No.1 Albums

1982	*SELECT*

SELECT topped the chart for one week.

Albums with the most weeks

29 weeks	*THE SINGLES COLLECTION 1981-1993*
26 weeks	*CLOSE*

14 weeks	*KIM WILDE*
10 weeks	*SELECT*
8 weeks	*LOVE MOVES*
8 weeks	*NEVER SAY NEVER*

KIM WILDE IN NEW ZEALAND

Only one of Kim's albums, *KIM WILDE*, has charted in New Zealand. It peaked at no.39, and spent two weeks on the chart.

KIM WILDE IN NORWAY

Kim has achieved four hit albums in Norway, which spent 52 weeks on the chart.

Her most successful album is *ANOTHER STEP*, which peaked at no.2.

Albums with the most weeks

16 weeks	*ANOTHER STEP*
15 weeks	*SELECT*
15 weeks	*CLOSE*
6 weeks	*LOVE MOVES*

KIM WILDE IN SOUTH AFRICA

None of Kim's albums have charted in South Africa.

KIM WILDE IN SWEDEN

Kim has achieved 10 hit albums in Sweden, which spent 131 weeks on the chart.

No.1 Albums

1981	*KIM WILDE*

KIM WILDE topped the chart for two weeks.

Albums with the most weeks

32 weeks	*CLOSE*
30 weeks	*KIM WILDE*
18 weeks	*SELECT*
12 weeks	*CATCH AS CATCH CAN*
10 weeks	*TEASES & DARES*
10 weeks	*THE SINGLES COLLECTION 1981-1993*

KIM WILDE IN SWITZERLAND

Kim has achieved 14 hit albums in Switzerland, which spent 132 weeks on the chart.

Her most successful album is *ANOTHER STEP* which peaked at no.5.

Albums with the most weeks

36 weeks	*CLOSE*
16 weeks	*CATCH AS CATCH CAN*
15 weeks	*LOVE IS*
10 weeks	*THE SINGLES COLLECTION 1981-1993*
9 weeks	*TEASES & DARES*
9 weeks	*LOVE MOVES*
9 weeks	*NEVER SAY NEVER*
8 weeks	*ANOTHER STEP*
7 weeks	*COME OUT AND PLAY*

KIM WILDE IN THE USA

Kim has achieved three Top 100 albums on the Billboard 200 in the United States, which spent 26 weeks on the chart.

Her most successful album is *ANOTHER STEP*, which peaked at no.40.

Albums with the most weeks

18 weeks	*ANOTHER STEP*
5 weeks	*KIM WILDE*
3 weeks	*TEASES & DARES*

RIAA (Recording Industry Association of America) Awards

The RIAA began certifying Gold albums in 1958, Platinum albums in 1976, and multi-Platinum albums in 1984. Gold = 500,000, Platinum = 1 million. Awards are based on shipments, not sales, and each disc is counted individually (so, for example, a double album has to ship 500,000 to be eligible for Platinum).

None of Kim's albums have been certified by the RIAA.

KIM WILDE IN ZIMBABWE

None of Kim's albums have charted in Zimbabwe.

Printed in Great Britain
by Amazon